BUSINESS
AND
THE ARTS

BUSINESS & THE ARTS

AN ANSWER TO TOMORROW

BY ARNOLD GINGRICH

FOREWORD BY DAVID ROCKEFELLER

Paul S. Eriksson, Inc., New York

A Business Committee for the Arts publication.

Grateful acknowledgment is made to the *New York Times* for permission to reprint the quotations appearing on pages 24, 30, 39, and 118, copyright 1967/68 by the New York Times Company; and to the *Wall Street Journal* for permission to reprint the quotations appearing on pages 31, 39, 85, 96, and 103, copyright 1968 by Dow Jones & Company, Inc.

THE BUSINESS COMMITTEE FOR THE ARTS
GRATEFULLY ACKNOWLEDGES
THE GENEROUS GRANT OF
THE HOWARD JOHNSON FOUNDATION
WHICH HAS HELPED MAKE POSSIBLE
THE PUBLICATION OF THIS WORK.

TABLE OF CONTENTS

LIST OF ILLUSTRATIONS

FOREWORD

by David Rockefeller

Almost imperceptibly over the past several years, the modern corporation has evolved into a social as well as an economic institution. Without losing sight of the need to make a profit, it has developed ideals and responsibilities going far beyond the profit motive. It has become, in effect, a full-fledged citizen, not only of the community in which it is headquartered but of the country and indeed the world.

The public has come to expect corporations to live up to certain standards of good citizenship. One of these is to help shape our environment in a constructive way. By environment I mean the vast complex of economic, technological, social and political forces that influence our cities and the people who live in them. In shaping this environment, the corporation must initiate its share of socially responsible action, rather than merely respond passively to outside forces.

Projects involving the arts are not just a kind of fluffy periphery of American life. They are an integral part of the solutions to the problems that face our country today. It is sadly evident that our cultural attainments have not kept pace with improvements in other fields. As people's incomes have risen, a proportionate share has not been devoted to artistic and intellectual pursuits. As leisure has increased, so has the amount of time given to unproductive and aimless activities. Corporations genuinely concerned about their environment cannot evade responsibility for seeing that there are more opportunities for a rewarding use of leisure time such as the arts provide.

At the same time we face the most serious crisis in our cities that we have ever known. We are asking our Congress and ourselves to make sacrifices in order to get at the root of the basic urban problems. Much of the solution is economic but it is broader than that. In addition to better lodging, better schooling, and a larger portion of the amenities of life, all of our people must share the beauty and creativity of our society.

The humanist revolution of mid-millennium Europe began with the Renaissance of the fourteenth to the sixteenth centuries. It was an era in which the dignity of the individual man was beginning to be recognized and celebrated to the world by the arts. What is man if his life is but to sleep and feed and work?, they cried. Now we are faced with the need to restate the importance of that individual for all the world to hear and see. Twentieth-century man with no interest outside his work can be as barren of sustaining hope as was the fourteenth-century serf tied to the land.

In our increasingly mechanized and computerized world, the arts illumine and reinforce our individuality through beauty and form and human emotion that can reach and move most men. They are indispensable to the achievement of our great and underlying concern for the individual: the fullest development of the potential hidden in every human being.

That, I submit, is our challenge and our responsibility.

Mr. Gingrich's book is a tangible and constructive contribution to the better understanding by us all of that challenge and how best to respond to it.

PREFACE

I compiled the speeches and other materials and wrote the original draft of this book during the summer of 1968 while ostensibly on vacation. It was, from the beginning of the exercise, a labor of love: I have long believed in the cause of corporate support for the arts.

It is impossible in so brief a work as this to make public record of all the good efforts of businessmen nationwide to help the arts. It has been necessary to select a few representative officers and corporations as typical. Although general support of the arts by business is still in its early stages, the roster of executives who not only believe but also are actively engaged in spreading the word is large enough to fill this volume merely with its listing. And it would in itself be a Blue Book of the top corporate personalities of this country. The infant movement of this support is growing apace, and this book will, because of the surge toward the necessary and inevitable corporate support of the arts, become within the next few years out of date, a curio of its day.

I am glad that this is so.

My thanks for their kind permission to quote widely from their writings and speeches are here gratefully given to Sam Cooper, Kenneth N. Dayton, C. Douglas Dillon, George M. Irwin, Dr. Charles F. Jones, Leo H. Schoenhofen, Dr. Frank Stanton and David Yunich. The Associated Councils of the Arts has been generous in its assistance in preparation of this book.

I am particularly indebted to W. Granville Meader, of the Business Committee for the Arts, for his help in editing the manuscript—a task for which he too took something of a busman's holiday—and his work on the Appendices, Bibliography and Index, which greatly enhance the volume's reference value.

New York, New York
November 1, 1968

ARNOLD GINGRICH

PART ONE:

THE BACKGROUND

THE RISE OF THE MOVEMENT

That business and the arts are not natural enemies is a latterday discovery. Before the 1965 publication of the Rockefeller Panel Report, *The Performing Arts: Problems and Prospects,* there was little general awareness of any relationship—other than the antithetical one implicit in such expressions as "Art and Mammon"—between business and the arts, and it was certainly not a topic of frequent discussion.

The keynote of a June, 1965 luncheon given by the New York Board of Trade at the Hotel Pierre was the rhetorical question, "Is Culture the Business of Business?" Obviously, the juxtaposition of terms was considered sufficiently novel to possess some shock value. That event marked the first recognition by the business community that there was a growing trend toward corporate support of the arts. At this affair, awards were given to twelve companies for activities in the arts, and to three companies for contributions to the environment through architectural accomplishments. The day was culminated by the formation of an Arts Advisory Council within the membership of this hundred-year-old Manhattan institution. A copy of the Rockefeller Panel Report was given to each of the more than five hundred persons present, and an awareness began to spread around the corporate world that the arts are a central, rather than a fringe, aspect of that society of which business now sees itself as an integral part.

That same month, in Washington, two arts-based organizations, the American Symphony Orchestra League and the Arts Councils of America (now the Associated Councils of the Arts), met in their then-joint annual conference, timed by coincidence to the moment of passage of the legislation establishing the National

Endowment for the Arts and the Humanities. There too, at the keynote luncheon, the subject was the Rockefeller Panel Report on the performing arts.

Due largely to the revelations of that report, some sense of interdependence between business and the arts began to take on general currency between the "two cultures," that of commerce and that of the muse. Before the year was over, something of a movement could be discerned.

By the next year, when the Twentieth Century Fund study, *Performing Arts: The Economic Dilemma,* by William J. Baumol and William G. Bowen, served to reinforce the growing realization that the arts could not be expected to be "a paying proposition," the movement had gained evident impetus. In the spring of '66, at a conference jointly sponsored by the New York Board of Trade and *Esquire* magazine, Theodore Sorenson sounded the keynote that "the business of business is America." The concept of corporate citizenship that had up until that point largely justified corporate support of the arts in narrow terms of "enlightened self-interest" began to be broadened, on the basis that "what's good for America is good for business."

To the rather passive corporate role of purely donative support of the arts, there was added the consideration of more active involvement, tending to the enlistment of the arts as an ameliorant of urban stresses in the short-term or tactical view, and as an enhancement of the quality of life in the community as a whole in the long-term or strategic view. It was decided to enlarge the scope of the New York-based Board of Trade "Business and the Arts" awards by adding *Esquire*'s "Business in the Arts" awards, in which the degree of community involvement is a determinant, quite apart from considerations of amounts of money or, for that matter, either size of the company or of the community.

Some idea of the momentum of the movement came with the realization that while it had taken some digging to come up with a dozen logical recipients of the

4

Board of Trade's 1965 awards, the judges of *Esquire*'s 1966 awards had close to two hundred nominations in hand.

The selection of twenty winners of *Esquire*'s 1966 awards was difficult for precisely the opposite problem of choosing a dozen winners for the Board of Trade awards the year before. Formerly there had been only a few. Within the year there were many.

By 1967, which saw the publication of *The Corporation and the Arts,* by Richard Eells, there were so many companies engaged in arts-related activities across the land that it was no longer possible for the judges to confine themselves to twenty selections. They had to enlarge the number, by the addition of Honorable Mentions, to forty-four.

Thus, a practice that had seemed unusual only a few years earlier was becoming regarded as commonplace.

But the real breakthrough came as the result of another Rockefeller activity. In 1966, at the Fiftieth Anniversary Conference of the National Industrial Conference Board, David Rockefeller, in a speech entitled "Culture and the Corporation," called for the creation of a committee to stimulate corporate support of the arts, patterned on the highly successful Council for Financial Aid to Education which, in fifteen years' activity, brought corporate support of education to more than $300 million annually from the previous token $55 million.

Actually, the Rockefeller Panel Report had suggested this type of committee in print the year before, but it was not until David Rockefeller renewed the plea *viva voce* that anything actually happened. In the fall of 1967 the Business Committee for the Arts was established under the chairmanship of former Secretary of the Treasury C. Douglas Dillon and the presidency of G. A. McLellan. It is comprised now of almost 100 business leaders across the country who participate by invitation.

5

This development was as important as the New York Board of Trade's pioneering move in the field just a couple of years earlier. Both concepts sprang from within the business community. It could now, with BCA established, be said that the business and the arts phenomenon, already remarkable for the speed with which it had caught on, was gaining national momentum.

PRESENT CORPORATE PARTICIPATION

According to the National Industrial Conference Board, civic and cultural causes together received only 3 per cent of corporate contributions a decade ago; now the total for the arts alone is 3 per cent. But that is nowhere near enough.

All figures in the national picture of the arts needs are at best good estimates. The Rockefeller Panel Report estimated the annual dollar gap between income and outgo of the performing arts alone as being between $40 and $60 million, but all subsequent studies have indicated that even the higher of those two figures was considerably low. The figures for art museums are simply not available. However, every study, including that of Baumol and Bowen on the performing arts and the museum report conducted by the American Association of Museums, points to the growing income gap and the critical financial needs of the arts. Furthermore, national figures are not necessary to make the point of need to any businessman involved with an arts organization struggling—as almost all of them are—for survival.

In considering the problems facing the arts, the 1966 New York Board of Trade Conference at Lincoln Center posited as a goal that if business could allocate to the arts one half of one per cent of the tax-deductible giving, it would raise the level of corporate support of the arts to around two hundred fifty million dollars yearly, a more than tenfold increase in the amount of giving then earmarked for the arts.

Although corporate contributions of all kinds (religion, health, education and welfare, as well as civic and cultural) may be taken on a tax-deductible basis up to a total of 5 per cent of income (see p. 67), John H. Watson, III of the National Industrial Conference Board has noted that while corporate contributions of all

Two views of Lincoln Center for the Performing Arts, New York.

kinds have been rising, their increase has been simply a reflection of rising corporate income, not of an increased *percentage* of income. Corporate philanthropy has remained approximately 1%, despite a fifty per cent rise (from around $530 million to $800 million in the years '62 to '65) in the amount of giving. There have been some spectacular examples of business gifts to the arts in recent years. American Export and Isbrandtsen Lines gave the Metropolitan the cost of a new production of "Aida." Eastern Air Lines gave a half million to the Metropolitan Opera in 1967 for a new production of the Wagnerian *Ring* cycle. TWA gave a hundred fifty thousand in 1967 to help meet the overseas touring expenses of the New York Philharmonic in 1969. These examples—outstanding as they are—are almost insignificant in raising the share of corporate contribution to the arts, when measured against the rise in corporate giving as a whole.

Even the available figures are subject to some guesswork, since most breakdowns of charitable giving lump "civic and cultural" together. Contributions in these fields rose, between 1962 and 1965, from 5.3 per cent to 8.3 per cent of all corporate giving. This has since led the National Industrial Conference Board to subdivide the category in its figures.

Money is in any case only a part of the story of business and the arts. That aspect of the relationship, the whole question of *support,* is merely a passive one. The question of involvement is the active side and, undoubtedly in the long run, the more fruitful for both partners in what Professor Eells terms "the business-arts nexus." For it presupposes not that one gives and the other takes, but that they enrich each other, while doing much for the community they share.

In all probability the level of business support of the arts will not rise to the indicated optimum level unless and until a greater degree of business involvement with the arts brings it about as a natural consequence, rather than as a result of high-pressure fundraising or the earnest exhortations of high level do-gooders. This is the point that was made back in 1965 by Frank Stanton of CBS, another stalwart of the movement, a point that has been too often lost sight of since.

The arm has been put on business often enough, purely in terms of seeking its support, during the drives for the proliferation of the cultural centers across the land. A pause is indicated, if only by the most elementary considerations of politeness, before the hat is passed on behalf of the attractions needed to people all those manifestations of the edifice complex, now that their actual construction is in some instances already assured.

Besides, businesses will be of a lot more help to the arts when their interest is volunteered rather than drafted. The businessman who involves his business with the arts because his own interest has been quickened by them, is likely to bring about a much deeper and more lasting relationship than the one who is dragooned into paying them lipservice and giving them no more than token support. In fact, without such involved men, it is doubtful that the business and the arts relationship would ever have become more than a biological sport, a rare and atypical phenomenon.

When Walter Paepcke, over forty years ago, transformed his family business into the Container Corporation of America, he took a giant step into the future of corporate evolution. His acts would have made him a leader, had he lived, even today.

First, he sought to give the company a new look that would benefit his ambitious conception of it as a national leader in the art of packaging. He did this by design, using the term in both its figurative and literal meaning. He made the Container Corporation synonymous with the best in modern design, boldly overstepping the limits of the conventional decorative devices of the time and venturing into the realm of the fine arts. The result was an almost overnight transformation of a staid outfit making a prosaic product into a pace-setting and trail-blazing new force in merchandising. It was as startling as the emergence of a butterfly from a cocoon.

Outside his office he was equally venturesome. He transformed a barren Colorado backwoods, many miles from nowhere, into an oasis of business enlightenment, with the establishment of the still-flourishing Aspen Institute for Humanistic Studies. Certainly if any one man could be said to have been the precursor of three such latterday phenomena as the "culture boom," "business in the arts," and "the corporation as citizen," that man would be Walter Paepcke. Today his like would not be hard to find, but looking back across four decades to his day, he towers out of the past like a beacon on a dark night.

But if Paepcke stands alone at the beginning, the name that since has lighted the path at every important juncture is Rockefeller. The Rockefeller Foundation gave the grant in 1954 that served as a life-preserving transfusion for the American Symphony Orchestra League, thus enabling it to wetnurse the infant community arts councils movement. Nelson Rockefeller, as Governor, with the formation of the New York State Council in 1960 gave the state arts councils movement its biggest single forward thrust towards its present eminence. Another Rockefeller, John D. 3rd, as chairman of the Rockefeller Panel launched that Sputnik, *The Performing Arts: Problems and Prospects,* that in 1965 dramatized the importance of the arts to American business much as the Soviet satellite in 1957 did that of science education. Yet another Rockefeller, David, by his activation of the Business Committee for the Arts in 1967 performed what may well appear, in another decade, to have been the most signal service ever done for the arts in America.

The point is that money isn't everything. It is hard sometimes, in looking back, to winnow the truth from the facts. Who can say now, with any certainty, that the Rockefeller Foundation money could have put the American Symphony Orchestra League on its feet in 1954 without a Helen Thompson, or that a Helen

Thompson could have done it without someone's interest in the Rockefeller Foundation that made the grant possible? It is probably enough to say that the first money that came in, when money was most needed, was the Rockefeller money. What is also remarkable, however, is how often that must be said, in any objective appraisal of the significant developments in the arts scene as a whole in our time.

The Ford Foundation, and especially W. McNeil Lowry's strategic role in determining the nature and placement of its benefactions, cannot go unnoticed in even the briefest of accounts of any aspect of the subject of support of the arts. Without it American ballet would be an even sorrier Cinderella figure, in relation to the other art forms, and the ranks of the nation's twenty-eight major and fifty-one metropolitan symphonies would undoubtedly have been decimated. Ford was the first of the foundations, in the fifties, to establish a truly comprehensive program in the arts. McNeil Lowry, at least as early as 1962, had in some of his speeches reached many of the conclusions about the problems and prospects of the performing arts emphasized later by the Rockefeller Panel Report.

Even with encouraging prospects of increased corporate support, and with such munificent aid as the 1965 Ford Foundation grant of $85 million for orchestras alone, it is obvious that the symphony and the opera, the dance and the theatre, the museum and educational television, those chronic mendicants, must resort to some form of Operation Bootstrap before their functional and congenital ailments are more than palliatively treated. Both the Baumol and Bowen study and the more recent Southern California Research Council Report, *The Challenge of Leisure,* project mounting income gaps, foreshadowing increased gloominess for an already somber picture.

In the decades when the annual deficit of the Boston Symphony was simply met by asking Major Henry Lee Higginson for a check, such emphasis on wooing the patrons outside the "Horseshoe Circle" would have been unthinkable, either for symphony or opera. But with the passing of the dominant single donor, selling the arts to a broader segment of the populace as a whole has become not only permissible but mandatory.

Whether or not the chronic income gap of the performing arts can ever be bridged, the arts can nevertheless benefit by applying business world techniques to the improvement of their operations and administration, without detriment to the quality or character of their product. This is the significance of case histories such as that of the Tyrone Guthrie Theatre in Minneapolis, as recounted in the wise and witty *In Search of an Audience,* by Bradley G. Morison and Kay Fliehr.

Corporate sales techniques have been applied successfully in Seattle, where a former Golden Gloves boxer, Glynn Ross, is selling opera, according to *The Wall Street Journal,* the way Madison Avenue sells beer, soap and automobiles. Ross, now general director of the Seattle Opera Association, has probably the only such organization in the nation giving out buttons proclaiming that "Opera Lives!" In four years of using such techniques, the Seattle Opera audience rose from 24,000 to 120,000 and its budget from $165,000 to $650,000. More importantly, ticket sales themselves cover more than half that budget, whereas the usual opera box office income meets between a quarter and a third of the costs. The 1968 Seattle Opera deficit was a miniscule $1,810.

What has become increasingly clear is that the support and involvement of business and the arts is far from being a one-way proposition, with all going out on the one hand and nothing coming in on the other. Business and the arts can have interdependent relations, without harm to either their autonomy or their identity, that can be of mutual benefit.

THE AMERICAN SYMPHONY ORCHESTRA LEAGUE

If the Associated Councils of the Arts (ACA) and the Business Committee for the Arts (BCA) represent two aspects of our direct and immediate concern, and they do, then it still would be less than fair to let the matter go so simply. To treat of the ACA without regard for the ASOL (The American Symphony Orchestra League) would be a shabby trick in view of the at least godmotherly relationship of the ASOL to the infant arts councils group before it was big enough to form an organization of its own. So perhaps the best way to consider the ACA, in perspective so to speak, is by way of the American Symphony Orchestra League.

Besides, the League is basic, in that the full orchestra embraces so many other forms, such as the components of chamber music groups and the orchestras that are fundamental to both opera and ballet. And because the League is so big and so well established, and had such a headstart in the whole arts field, it was in a position to mother more than one other now separate arts group. In addition to the ACA, both the Music Critics Association and the Music Committee of the People to People Program under the Eisenhower Administration, grew out of the League.

The ASOL has been in existence for over thirty-five years. It was established as a nonprofit organization, but before 1950 it was entirely a volunteer operation concerned almost exclusively with community orchestras. It was founded in Michigan in 1942 by Mrs. Leta Snow, the founder and manager of the Kalamazoo Symphony, together with a free-lance writer in Lansing, Miss Theresa Shire, who was interested in the subject of symphonies. In 1950, when the League still had only 72 members, Mrs. Helen M. Thompson, at that time the manager of the Charleston, (West Virginia) Symphony, was persuaded to become full-time ASOL executive secretary, to try to give the League a fresh start.

For the next four years, the League literally functioned as a cottage industry out of Helen Thompson's house. It wasn't until 1954, and the first of several Rockefeller Foundation grants, that the League's potential stature began to be realized. It then began its studies and surveys of the infant arts councils movement, taking the arts councils members into its own voting membership. Meanwhile the ASOL began to grow toward its present well-nigh all-inclusive membership of the nation's principal orchestras (between nine hundred and a thousand of the 1,450 orchestras of all sizes and kinds in the country).

In 1961, Mrs. Jouett Shouse gave the League its office building and land, on her Wolf Trap Farm fifteen miles west of Washington, D.C. The League was then incorporated as a nonprofit organization in the Commonwealth of Virginia and the following year received a Congressional nonprofit charter.

Throughout the fifties and early sixties, on the assumption that anything that helps the arts in general helps the symphony in particular, the League found itself devoting more and more time and attention and effort to general chore-boy duties for the arts as a whole, simply because people knew nowhere else to turn. There were constantly increasing demands on the League, not only from its own members but from every type of organization including federal government agencies, states, cities, libraries, the press, educational institutions, service agencies of all kinds, and even from foreign governments and service organizations. Every new development of the fast-changing arts field exerted some degree of change in the world of orchestras. The materialization of long-rumored federal arts programs, foundation interest, the expansion of the arts council concept which the League had done so much to foster, the increasing interest on the part of business and industry in participation in the arts and the expectation that a like boom in interest could be spawned with the labor unions, and above all the incredible expansion and extension of college and university musical activities with their consequent impingement upon community life—all these put unexpected and unanticipated demands on the League for extensive research, experimentation and service on a national basis.

With its heavy dependence on volunteer work, that had to be its own reward, it is remarkable that the League was able to expand its activities and continue to grow and at the same time function with much better than bureaucratic efficiency. Many a business organization with national distribution and sales could well envy the smoothness with which this largely, indeed predominantly, amateur organization manages to get things done and to keep its orchestra members mutually informed and advised, down to the smallest detail, of every managerial and administrative development and technique.

THE ASSOCIATED COUNCILS OF THE ARTS

The ACA story is intimately intertwined with that of the American Symphony Orchestra League in all but its relatively recent chapters, but these latter are of course the more interesting and exciting, for they represent the period of its greatest growth and importance.

While it must be considered citizen-based, its programs are directed to corporate leadership at the local and national level, and it does command an abundance of business ability through the board membership of such figures as George M. Irwin, R. Philip Hanes, Jr., Fred Lazarus III, Terry Sanford, and Harold L. Zellerbach.

Nancy Hanks of the Rockefeller Special Studies Projects, currently ACA president, has been involved in virtually every significant development in the business and the arts movement from the compilation of *The Performing Arts: Problems and Prospects* to the formation of the Business Committee for the Arts. These two events, at least so far, stand as the beginning and the peak of the business and the arts story.

The ACA established its national office in 1965 and has had fantastic growth reflecting that of the community and state councils themselves. Although the first community councils were formed in the late forties, the great majority of the six hundred presently in existence have been organized in recent years. During this period too the first federal arts agency, the National Endowment for the Arts, was established. The number of official state arts agencies increased so that there was one in each of the fifty states and four of the American territories, up from the handful that had been in existence prior to 1965.

The phenomenal growth of interest in the arts and the resulting development of the arts councils is attributed by Nancy Hanks to six separate pressures:

1. *Population growth: the U.S. has passed the 200 million mark, with 360 million projected by the century's end;*
2. *urbanization, with the U.S. present 65 per cent of city dwellers expected to reach 75 per cent by the century's end;*
3. *increased amount of leisure time calculated by Herman Kahn and Anthony Wiener in* The Year 2000 *as likely to total 218 free days a year for the average employee, with a consequent possible need to ration theatre and museum attendance;*
4. *increased attention to the arts in both our elementary and secondary educational curricula;*
5. *tremendous increase in the number of our young people obtaining college education, and the surprising factor that some 18 per cent of college students now evince a career interest in the creative arts;*
6. *record—and still rising—participation in the arts on an amateur basis.*

Add to these pressures the probable consequences of the already planned construction of more than one hundred cultural centers in urban areas all over the land, and throw in the influence of some 300 new arts organizations that were given tax-exempt status in the U.S. in the year 1966 alone. It is easy to see why the arts councils movement is one of the biggest booms, at least in percentage figures, that this continent has ever had.

R. Philip Hanes, Jr., a pioneer in the arts councils movement and ACA's president in the key year of 1965, has said that the arts councils "sprang from the dreams of their parents," the arts, and that their "foster parents" were the Junior League, the ASOL and the Rockefeller Foundation. Recalling the annual meetings held from 1955 on in conjunction with the conferences of the ASOL, Hanes characterized the first five years as a period of "searching growth" in which the arts councils tried to create a national organization whose purpose would be to assist, through the exchange of information, cooperative arts movements in both the United

States and Canada. During the period of 1960 to 1965 the national organization developed from a volunteer board to the full-time staff it now has, as it became evident that volunteers, no matter how dedicated, simply could not keep up with the demands of the increasing number of community arts councils, which "popped up like mushrooms after a summer rain" and immediately requested assistance. Some wrote six or eight pages of single-spaced typewritten letters; others wrote such single sentences as Tampa's "How do you start an arts council and build a cultural center?"

One of the staunchest of the original group of volunteers, Ralph Burgard, began as executive director of the Winston-Salem Arts Council. He is now director of state and community relations of ACA. He writes in his book, *Arts in the City,* also of the origins of the movement. The first privately incorporated arts councils, he says, were formed in the 1940s, and they numbered 75 in 1960 when the first state arts council was organized. Quincy, Illinois arts leaders, with George M. Irwin, a local businessman and symphony conductor, as chairman, founded the Quincy Society of Fine Arts in 1948, initially as a clearinghouse for adult and school art programs and to help local cultural groups. Later they set up a central office to provide management services to their organizations.

The Arts Council, Inc. of Winston-Salem was organized in 1949. Since that time, it has helped organize 7 new arts organizations, constructed an arts center and established a united arts fund. On one occasion, under the leadership of R. Philip Hanes, Jr., local businessmen raised more than $1 million in 48 hours for the North Carolina School of the Arts, a high school and college for the performing arts.

After a community-wide survey in 1950 recommended better facilities for the arts and development of new audiences, the St. Paul Council of Arts and Sciences was organized. When, in 1953, $1.7 million of a city bond issue was allocated for an arts and science center, a full-time director was hired.

These and other similar Burgard recollections of the grass-roots beginnings of

19

the nationwide arts councils movement give some idea of the problems and trends that the arts scene is currently undergoing. He is particularly cogent on the current functions and opportunities of arts councils in his book.

Several art forms, he says, are not yet broadly enough supported for sustained public performances in our cities. Most serious films are still presented on university campuses, before small film societies or in major metropolitan art-film houses. Our great modern dance companies, such as those directed by Martha Graham, Merce Cunningham and Paul Taylor, are still more widely acclaimed in Europe than in this country. Few in America yet appreciate such contemporary artists as Robert Rauschenburg, who are experimenting with the simultaneous use of several art forms: film, theater, television, kinetic sculpture and music, dance and technology, total environments. Most such experiments do not fit comfortably into areas traditionally served by existing arts institutions.

Arts councils should cooperate with other local institutions, Burgard says, to provide initial sponsorship for presentations in such experimental fields. They might thus stimulate public interest sufficiently to encourage local groups to sponsor further programs independently.

Arts councils could provide a new frame of reference for art and the city. They could help overcome the anti-intellectual tradition in America that gives the arts the ornamental status of a "leisure-time activity." Culture is not now generally regarded as a quality or insight found within the people, but as something tangible that one acquires at the concert hall or hangs on the walls at home.

Our American passion for orderliness tends to compress the arts into a few major institutional packages—*the* symphony, *the* museum, *the* theater—leaving everything else to community neglect. Arts councils must be concerned with the confrontation of *art* and people, not art *institutions* and people. "People in ghetto areas may need music but not symphony concerts, art but not exhibitions of Rembrandts."

Every arts council, adds Burgard, must still assist the major arts institutions in solving their enormous problems of finance, personnel and public education. Nevertheless, no arts council can ignore contemporary art and those who create it. One must live in the future to better understand the present. The artist's role is crucial to this insight. The workers in mixed media, together with the poets, painters, composers, choreographers and playwrights, must be encouraged. Their essential role in society must be made clearer to the public, he concludes, even if their works remain largely misunderstood.

The chances are that the average businessman can understand the sense of Burgard's statement a lot faster than the average person without business experience. Every businessman who has a line of regular models to sell knows that its acceptance is given help of a "lead-cow" sort by the inclusion of a few advanced, extreme or frankly experimental numbers at the top end of the line. They may not sell, but they help sell the regular line. Without them, the average customer might find *that* too advanced or extreme.

Ever since attaining its own autonomy as a national organization, ACA has done the same kind of overall comprehensive job for the arts as a whole, on the metropolitan and the regional level, that the American Symphony Orchestra League has done for the musical scene, and the range and extent of its activities have been steadily broadening. Publications have included the proceedings of its annual conferences and recently the Morison-Fliehr book, *In Search of an Audience,* already mentioned, as well as the Burgard *Arts in the City.* Since late 1967, the ACA has produced the quarterly, *Cultural Affairs,* a magazine designed to provide arts councils with their own journal covering subjects of interest and value to them. Its scope is actually much broader. As the only national quarterly covering all the arts it can be read with enjoyment and reward by anyone interested in the cultural life of North America.

Other projected ACA publishing projects are a study on labor relations in the performing arts by Dr. Michael Moskow, associate professor of economics at Temple University, and a book on the planning of arts centers by Peter Blake, editor of *Architectural Forum*.

In the few years of its existence as a national organization, ACA has done a remarkable job. It has helped the councils obtain the expertise they need in arts administration, legislative relations, fund-raising, programming and public relations, conducting workshops and seminars both independently and in cooperation with state and community arts councils and local arts organizations. Its administration seminars for state arts councils have been especially valuable, because this is such a new field that there is a critical shortage of personnel with any form of training in arts management. Its national conferences alternate between small institutional seminars and large public forums for all the arts.

Through its arts information service and the facilities of its library (actually the only one in the country on the management and financing of the arts), ACA has been able to assist both state and community councils in the attainment of meaningful agenda where without them they would have had to grope blindly. ACA has also shown the benefit of its years of early association with the American Symphony Orchestra League, for it has extended to other arts forms a great deal of the good business "housekeeping" that the League has long since made familiar to the orchestral scene.

ACA must also be credited with the first truly business-like approach to one of the immemorial problems of the performing arts, the chronic gap between audience revenue and performance costs. This has been faced up to sensibly and realistically in the Morison-Fliehr book, commissioned by the ACA and made possible by a grant from Shell Companies Foundation.

ACA has here shown not only that its heart is in the right place, but also that its head is level and its feet are on the ground, for this book is, as Oliver Rea says of it in the Foreword, a concentrated attack on the major problem facing the performing arts in this country today. It is also, as Sir Tyrone Guthrie says of it in the Preface, reflective of a deeper humanity and wider horizon than are usually associated with those whose task is to publicize and sell. Morison and Mrs. Fliehr sum up the chief problem of the performing arts very well in the conclusion of their book when they say of the necessity of increased support of the arts:

> ... *The question then arises in our minds whether such support will be given to institutions that serve only a highly select three or four per cent of the population ... There is necessity, as we believe, to seek ways to make audiences reflective of a cross-section of society ... The existing image of the arts is a formidable obstacle to enlarging and broadening audiences. It is far too high-society, long-haired intellectual, artsy and sissy in our opinion.*
>
> *In order to broaden and enlarge audiences, artistic institutions must penetrate the Cultural Curtain. They must find ways to communicate with the majority of the population who will not listen because they have been intimidated into believing the arts are not for them.*

While it is directly concerned with the problem of building an audience for repertory theater, the work contains many guidelines that are equally applicable to the audience problems of all arts organizations—the symphony, opera, dance, theater and museums.

Morison and Mrs. Fliehr are speaking for themselves of course, and generalizing out of their specific experience over the first four years of the Tyrone Guthrie Theatre in Minneapolis, but they are also speaking for and through ACA.

THE BUSINESS COMMITTEE FOR THE ARTS

The Business Committee for the Arts (BCA), the youngest of the organizations, was formed in the fall of 1967 and has been fully functional only since the spring of 1968. But this group signifies the coming of age of the business and the arts movement. It appeared as though in response to a June, 1967 *New York Times* editorial entitled "Money and the Muse," which said in part: "The days when a wealthy patron . . . made up the deficits are over. Large-scale help from government is not imminent. The corporations are the principal remaining and virtually untapped source." Actually, of course, the formation of such a body as the BCA was called for as far back as the spring of 1965, by the Rockefeller Panel Report, which asked for "an organization patterned on the Council for Financial Aid to Education" which would "be useful in stimulating corporate support for the arts."

David Rockefeller made the suggestion specific in 1966 at the Fiftieth Anniversary Conference of the National Industrial Conference Board:

> *Such a Council, drawn from the ranks of businessmen knowledgeable in the arts, cultural leaders and representative artists, could provide strong impetus and clearly defined direction for what is often rather haphazard progress.*
>
> *As I see it, this organization would devote itself to broadening the base of corporate support through four main avenues.*
>
> *First, it would conduct research on a national basis to provide statistical analyses of the voluntary support being generated on behalf of the arts. These reports would furnish an authoritative yardstick for the appraisal of the progress being made in this area.*

Second, it would provide expert counseling for business firms seeking to initiate new programs or expand existing ones. Such counseling could range from comprehensive program analyses and recommendations to special detailed treatment of varied kinds of aid.

Third, it would carry on a nationwide program of public information to keep corporations informed of opportunities that exist in the arts, and to apprise the artistic community of what corporations are doing in their particular fields.

Fourth, it would work to increase the effectiveness of cultural organizations in obtaining voluntary support from business and industry, and to encourage the involvement of more businessmen as trustees of cultural groups.

Quite frankly, it has been my observation that some cultural organizations don't always make the most intelligent and forceful case for themselves when they seek corporate support. Their reasoning is often fuzzy, their documentation fragile. Even the most public-spirited corporation has, I think, a right to expect the organization seeking its help to prove that it has competent management, a realistic budget and workable plans to attain immediate objectives as well as long-range goals.

I feel it would be enormously helpful for representatives of business and the arts to exchange views face to face, to seek new ideas from each other, to clarify misunderstandings and explore new possibilities. It would help bridge the gap between the sometimes rigid mentality of the businessman and the creative spirit of the artist. Both sides could benefit far more from constructive critical interest than from biased attack or hostile neglect.

Of necessity, the concept of a Council on Business and the Arts must be outlined here in its broadest terms. Yet I would hope that the basic idea has sufficient validity to justify further exploration of its possibilities.

When more than 200 letters from top businessmen across the country enthusiastically endorsed his idea, the staffs of the National Industrial Conference

Board and the Rockefeller Brothers Fund began the essential organizational activities. A founding committee was established including, besides C. Douglas Dillon as chairman, Roger Blough, chairman of the United States Steel Corporation; Katharine Graham, president of the Washington Post Company; Devereux Josephs, director of the New York Life Insurance Company; Gavin MacBain, chairman of the Bristol-Myers Company; H. Bruce Palmer, president of the National Industrial Conference Board; and Mr. Rockefeller. Subsequently 80 business leaders accepted membership in the Business Committee for the Arts. They represented 21 different types of industry, from airlines to banks to textile, with home offices in 37 cities across the United States, including Honolulu and Ponce, Puerto Rico. In mid-1968 membership was expanded by invitation to 94. Now representing 42 cities, BCA is truly a valid cross-section of the American corporate structure.

At the inaugural meeting of BCA, at the Metropolitan Museum of Art in New York in January, 1968, David Rockefeller keyed the BCA rationale closely to the interest of the times:

> *What this Committee is seeking to do is not something that can be given third, or fourth or fifth priority either to ourselves or to our companies or to the country. It is of vital importance now. If we, as a Committee, can contribute to bringing about in America a renaissance of beauty and creativity and greatness in culture, we will have made a significant contribution to our country and toward solving problems that seem in one sense so remote from the arts and in another so close to them.*

Gifts of $50,000 each from John D. Rockefeller 3rd and David Rockefeller provided "seed" money for the Committee when it was first formed, enabling it to acquire facilities and staff to begin operations. With that, BCA president G. A. McLellan moved his small staff into modest quarters in New York and proceeded to seek further funding for the operation. In October, 1968, Chairman Dillon announced that BCA had received grants from foundations totalling an additional $725,000, sufficient funding for the first three years of the Committee's activities, through December 31, 1970. Douglas Dillon said the grants afford BCA adequate resources and time in which to demonstrate the value to American business and industry of the programs approved at the Committee's inaugural meeting.

Commitments of support have been made by the following foundations: Rockefeller Brothers Fund, $225,000; Old Dominion Foundation, $75,000; Ford Foundation, a nonrenewable grant of $225,000; and the Rockefeller Foundation, $200,000. The first three grants cover a three-year period. The Rockefeller Foundation grant may be drawn from at the rate of $75,000 per year, but it may also be apportioned over a period of four years.

Douglas Dillon said he was gratified by the confidence in the Committee's program expressed by these grants. He added that BCA would use the funds to conduct a broad range of communications activities to interest business organizations in assuming a significant share of responsibility for support of the arts. The need for such support has been amply documented in recent studies, but it has not been well publicized outside the arts community. Some businesses, large and small, have participated closely and beneficially in arts programs of one kind or another, but effective channels through which other companies might profit from their experience have hitherto been unavailable. BCA will disseminate information and ideas on all phases of business involvement in arts programs through publications, seminars, lectures and the mass media. It hopes, through such efforts, to bring the art and business communities into close and fruitful relations with one another.

Douglas Dillon said the Committee is convinced that the arts are as important to a healthy business environment as education and health. If we permit the arts to become enfeebled through lack of support, the result can only be a general impoverishment of the spirit that will depress the values that sustain our society.

27

There is a great deal that the Committee can do to increase the number and value of alliances of the arts and business without directly dealing with funds for any specific group. BCA's primary functions are evangelical, to establish a climate. It plans through its publications, conferences, research and the promotion of examples to awaken American business to the same generous and steady acceptance of its responsibilities to the arts as it has accepted over the past fifteen years in its support of higher education. That it is already active in its evangelical function can be seen from the accomplishments described below:

The *BCA News,* a quarterly four-page newsletter, is distributed to more than 8,000 addressees, including all presidents of American companies with more than $1 million in assets and more than 500 employees. The publication highlights specific examples of business support of the arts. Some articles specify ways in which representatives of the business community and arts groups are working actively together. The rationale that business should support cultural activities on a local as well as a national basis is emphasized. Factual materials from available studies and publications are synthesized in graphic form.

In recognition of the need to communicate through the spoken as well as the written word, Committee members have been asked to join a Speakers Bureau, promising to make one or two speeches a year at carefully selected meetings across the nation. Nearly half the members have agreed to this, and as many other company executives and others interested in stimulating corporate support of the arts have offered their services.

Informal, one-day seminars are scheduled across the country to stimulate dialogue between business and arts leaders. Attendance is limited to thirty persons or fewer, half drawn from business, half the arts. Normally, a Committee member is in attendance and a Committee member's company is host.

A member of the BCA staff works with a local business leader in making arrangements and plans. Representatives of business discuss the cultural climate in their community and those requests for support which they have received. At the same time, they provide constructive guidance to arts representatives. Arts leaders are asked to avoid using the sessions as an occasion to request aid. Rather, they are asked to regard them as an opportunity to establish rapport with the people who can advise them, and to consider in common with business leaders how best their problems can be solved.

These meetings also serve as a source of information to be incorporated in a BCA handbook or guide to arts organizations seeking business support.

BCA has asked fifteen members of large corporations to constitute an Informal Advisory Group on whom the BCA staff may call on a regular or *ad hoc* basis to review proposed projects, research programs, etc., and to offer suggestions. Members of this group, representing the largest corporations in the United States, work closely with BCA in its day-to-day operations.

On March 20, 1968, a few months after its formation, Howard Taubman, in *The New York Times,* characterized BCA's tactics and pace as low pressure. He wondered, for instance, why the Committee hadn't made more attempts to attract public notice when it was formed, or why it hadn't used its first full meeting at the Metropolitan to make a big splash, and he asked this of Devereux C. Josephs, the former head of the New York Life Insurance Company and the treasurer of BCA.

"We weren't even sure until we'd met," said Josephs, "that we mightn't break up at once. One man who had joined the Committee warned us that he's against business support of the arts, that he believes only in private support. But he's active. If he turns out to be a devil's advocate, we can use that, too."

Taubman asked Douglas Dillon whether he thought that the new generation of business leaders might be more sophisticated and responsive to the arts. Douglas Dillon replied that this was possible. He said he believed that the business community was, like the nation as a whole, more aware than in earlier decades that the performing and visual arts were valuable to the quality of life. What's more, he added, business leaders are learning to tolerate the kind of existence and differences of opinion and taste the arts generate.

Did the Committee intend to press its own members to have their companies set an example?

"We will not press anyone," said Douglas Dillon, "but we hope to find ways to get leadership. There has been such leadership in the creation of new institutions like the Lincoln Center for the Performing Arts and the Los Angeles Music Center. What we need is to develop the habit of giving regularly and increasingly for established and new artistic efforts."

Were the Committee never to attract another line of space, BCA would richly justify its existence if it did nothing more than implement Douglas Dillon's avowed aim, as expressed in the Taubman interview above mentioned, "to develop the habit of giving regularly and increasingly for established and new artistic efforts."

The Council for Financial Aid to Education, after which BCA was patterned, has never become known as a headline-grabber, but its performance can well be likened to the Theodore Roosevelt motto of "Speak softly and carry a big stick." In the same March 20, 1968 story about the BCA, Howard Taubman summarized it neatly:

"Mr. Dillon and his colleagues have not fixed a money goal, but are convinced that giving must be multiplied many times. They would like to see business rally significantly to the arts, as it did to higher education in the last decade. Then, thanks to the efforts of a similar business committee, contributions rose from a few millions to the hundreds of millions."

John J. O'Connor, in an April 5, 1968 story in *The Wall Street Journal,* referred to BCA as "determinedly quiet" and gave as one of its envisioned accomplishments the setting up of "a business complement to the arts councils already existing (but hardly operating with uniform efficiency) in all states of the union." He added that until recently the idea of a BCA would have been unthinkable. However, there has been an unmistakable although gradual broadening of the corporation's "enlightened self-interest" approach to involvement in public affairs during the past ten or fifteen years. After citing numerous examples of the now generally acknowledged awareness of the corporation's social responsibility to the community, O'Connor pointed out that there are areas where such self-interest, in essence assuring that corporate outlays for outside purposes also bring economic benefits to the corporation, still persists widely. "This year the burning interest is the racial question," he added, and "the implied thesis is, no racial tension, no support." The entire approach assumes a tinge of irrelevancy in the picture of national culture.

Beyond question, there is a good deal of truth in this. In *Esquire*'s Business in the Arts award competitions we came across more than one instance where companies that had previously been active in the support of cultural projects had now switched the allocation of their philanthropies entirely to the realm of direct concern with urban problems. But it is equally beyond question that since the habit of giving has if anything been stimulated rather than diminished by the urgency of the problems connected with unrest in the cities, the arts will in the long run wind up winner. The big thing, as Douglas Dillon pointed out in the Howard Taubman interview, is to develop the habit of giving, regularly and increasingly.

Douglas Dillon might have answered Taubman's question, about the increased responsiveness of the new generation of business leaders to the arts, with this quote from Dr. Frank Stanton, president of CBS and one of his own Com-

31

*J. Irwin Miller's Cummins Engine Foundation paid the architect's fees for Harry Weese &
Associates to design the First Baptist Church, Columbus, Indiana.*

mittee's members, in a speech he made to the Arts Council of Columbus, Ohio, his home town:

> *There is a new breed of American arising, and it is a breed in league with the arts. When I was in college, a microscopic proportion of colleges and universities had art collections or museums or performing arts curricula. But things are changing. The university is not only a center of the humanities and the sciences today—it is a center of the arts, too. The rise in the number of graduate degrees granted in the fine arts—from 105 in 1940 to 4,672 in 1965—represents an increase of nearly 4,400 per cent. And of all college and university art museums, two-thirds have been established in the last 20 years. They are being used, up to the hilt, not just by art majors but by all the students—those who are going to furnish the leadership tomorrow . . . for business. This coming generation is not going to be at home in an environment that says that the only concern of business is the 30-day balance sheet. They are going to relate the stewardship of business, as I believe they should, to a sharpened awareness of the environment in which it functions.*

Not every member of BCA necessarily shares every view expressed by Stanton, but certainly he is not atypical of the new breed of businessman heavily represented in the Business Committee for the Arts.

Neither, for that matter, is J. Irwin Miller, of Cummins Engine Company, who has turned his small home town, Columbus, Indiana, into an oasis of architectural distinction. He is a highly successful businessman, director of a half dozen corporations. He is a graduate of Yale and Oxford and—a far more unusual distinction today—a current reader of Latin and Greek, with a Jeffersonian interest in architecture—he has two Saarinen houses himself. For relaxation, he plays Bach on his Stradivarius. As a businessman, he undoubtedly is atypical, as he is not only an active civil-rights supporter—he helped organize the March On Washington—but he also

33

harbors the bizarre belief that business should help government in the revolutionary attainment of goals that have so far characterized only the welfare state. He not only gives away a measurable portion of his own wealth but actually went to court for the right to do the same on behalf of two of his children.

The difference that men like many of the members of BCA can make in all our lives was well expressed by Harold Howe II, U.S. Commissioner of Education, (now vice president, Ford Foundation), at Ohio State University in June of 1967, when he said that we have paid a heavy price for our national sense that being rugged, virile and modern is somehow opposed to the notion of caring about beauty in our lives. If a concern for aesthetics had been infused into large numbers of Americans fifty years ago, we would not have so much squalor and ugliness in our cities and towns today.

We need greater numbers of corporation presidents, he said, who believe there's something more to building a new plant than finding the lowest cost per square foot. We need taxpayers who believe that if we're going to put up public housing, we might as well do it right, and erect handsome structures that will still be goodlooking twenty years from now, rather than replace slum tenements with more modern slums. We need a generation of Americans with a sharpened sense of taste and a concern for excellence in every aspect of their lives.

PART TWO:
THE RATIONALE

INTRODUCTION

Why business should support the arts, and the ways it can benefit, either immediately or ultimately, by doing so, has engaged the attention of a number of corporate spokesmen since the publication of the Rockefeller Panel Report on the performing arts first gave the question sufficent currency to make it of general interest.

Only a very few companies have approached the federally-approved five per cent deductible contribution. The Cummins Engine Company and the Dayton Corporation are notable exceptions. They have for years donated the full five per cent of their pretax profits to charitable institutions and worthy causes. But the average corporation across the country consistently contributes only slightly more than one per cent.

Contributions to the arts are good business. This has been proved over and over again during the past few years, and the speeches of the corporate executives which follow emphasize the fact.

Arts projects bring additional money to the community, give employment and enhance the community's prestige. No one has yet made a careful study of the financial blow to New York if the theatres were to close permanently—restaurants, taxis, ticket brokers, costume and stage set rental shops, newspaper advertising, not to mention department stores which sell clothing to theater patrons. The loss would clearly run into the millions of dollars. But here are some minor items which indicate that across the country the arts really do mean business:

ITEM: The Saratoga, New York, Performing Arts Center brought two million dollars in increased business to the community in two summer months its first

Above: Kaiser Industries' Kaiser Center Roof Garden, Oakland, California.

Below: Dorothy Chandler Pavilion, The Music Center of the County of Los Angeles.

year of operation, and one businessman reported sales 21% above normal for the period.

ITEM: The failing Stockbridge, Mass., summer theater was saved by the local bank because so many houses were rented after the opening of the theater.

ITEM: The new Oakland, California, Art Museum will bring an additional ten million tourist dollars per year, according to Kaiser Industries estimates.

ITEM: Since the establishment of the Tyrone Guthrie Theater there, many more tourists stop to spend two or three days and some dollars in Minneapolis to see their dramatic productions.

ITEM: The State of Utah is helping underwrite out-of-state tours by the Utah Symphony Orchestra as a means of influencing leading corporations to relocate in the state. One result was the decision of General Instruments to build an electronics facility in Salt Lake City.

ITEM: The Lancaster, Pennsylvania, County Industrial Development Bureau recently advertised in *The Wall Street Journal:* "Consider the Advantages of a Town with America's Oldest Living Theatre."

ITEM: The Southern Company of Atlanta, Georgia and Birmingham, Alabama, recently took a full-page color advertisement in the *Saturday Review* to declare: "Frank Mattox came to Alabama to head a new automotive parts plant. He and his wife got a lot in the bargain. . . . At the university in nearby Tuscaloosa, attractions such as the resident Cadek String Quartet complement a fine academic program."

ITEM: In New York, "a stable economy, the development of new office building, *a rebirth of culture and entertainment facilities,* and an ever-growing inclination for leisure-time activities have created a bright environment for retail business." —*New York Times,* November 1, 1967. (Emphasis added.)

In the first phase of the business and the arts movement, the prevalent theme

39

was "enlightened self-interest," and it was fairly narrowly bounded by considerations, whether explicit or implicit, of "what's in it for me?" But in the later, more sophisticated stage, such considerations, while not entirely absent, have become much less readily apparent, as the relationship of business and the arts progresses from support to involvement.

Donative support is tactical; participation is strategic. As such, they may be progressive stages of a company's relationship to the arts, but they are by no means mutually exclusive terms. There is room for both, within the working rationale that is evolving for business and the arts.

In the instances that follow, both in this Part and the next, examples may be found of both donative support and participation. It is only natural, since this book derives so largely from the beginnings of a movement that is still so young although fast growing, that the element of involvement is much less frequently encountered than that of support.

To establish the rationale of why business should support and become involved in the arts, I have in a sense asked corporate leaders to speak for themselves. Here are extracts from six talks by as many executives, talks given in a half-dozen different cities before widely varying audiences from arts groups to hard-to-persuade businessmen. All of the speeches were given after the publication of the Rockefeller Panel Report in 1965, and yet all have much in common with that Report—a feeling of the urgency of inducing corporate awareness of the importance of the arts in present-day society.

Here, in neither chronological nor alphabetical order, are the voices of today's American corporate executives, each varying from the others, yet all agreeing.

THE ARTS AND CORPORATE CITIZENSHIP

Will the businesses of the future live up fully to their responsibility of corporate citizenship? In order to pursue this question I would like to explore briefly the relationship between business and the arts.

On the surface, business and the arts have very little in common. Business is concerned (so it is said) primarily with its own preservation. The prime purpose of most corporations is to earn the maximum profit for the shareholders. To be sure, most businesses want to be good citizens, but by nature they must be practical and hardheaded.

The arts are just the opposite. Their primary goal is less practical, more visionary and vague. The arts are involved in a search for truth and beauty, for happiness and well-being. And at their best the arts can give society a sense of higher values and loftier standards.

What then do these two opposites have in common? For one thing, increasingly the same men are running both. Or at least the men who are running the one are lending increasing support to the other. For it is true that the arts are no longer the province of the princes, the idle rich, the effete.

Fortunately, business is beginning to realize this and is beginning to support the arts in a significant, if hesitant, way. Perhaps business is realizing that if it doesn't do the job, the government will. As is always the case, where there is a need and a demand from the public, and where private initiative fails, the government will fill the void.

Increasingly, successful executives realize that there is something more to living than pure business success. There is something beyond money and power and

Extract of remarks by Kenneth N. Dayton, executive vice president, Dayton Corporation, to deans of college business administration schools, Minneapolis, October 19, 1967

41

influence and achievement. There is an obligation to help build a better society. Building a successful business or a fabulous career in an unhealthy and unwholesome environment is somehow becoming less and less rewarding. It is indeed a hollow accomplishment.

Perhaps my company and I are cases in point. I spend a great deal of my business and leisure time working for the Minneapolis Symphony Orchestra.

I do it for two reasons. First, because I love the orchestra, and I get tremendous enjoyment and stimulation from great music. Second, because it is one of the community's greatest assets. I am convinced that we have a unique opportunity to build here one of the world's great orchestras.

Dayton Corporation lets me do it because, like many other Twin Cities corporations, it believes that the best way to make its business grow in this community is to help the community grow.

Because of our strong feeling that environmental factors will have as much to do with our success as merchandising and operating decisions, we have organized our business to help build a better community.

We annually contribute 5% of our income before taxes for charitable and civic purposes. We think to do so is in the best long-term interest of our stockholders.

It seems to me that one of the great tragedies of the private enterprise system is that so few American corporations have taken advantage of this great opportunity which the federal government has given them.

In essence the government has said to American business, "If you will build a better community, we will pay half the bill and let you call the tune." We are in an age of bigness and centralization. Unless the giant corporations of America step up to this opportunity and obligation, they may well find that the government will do the whole job (or at least try to do it), and then will increase corporate and individual taxes to pay the additional cost.

Progress is being made, if painfully slowly. The question is, will it come fast enough to give the arts the kind of support they desperately need to flourish in this country? Progress could be much faster if more business leaders could only recognize that the overriding purpose of the free enterprise system is not merely to preserve itself or to make the maximum profit, but to serve society.

Unless business recognizes that its primary goal is to serve society, it undoubtedly cannot survive as we know it. The means to this goal is maximum long-range profit, but we must not confuse the means with the end.

Maximum long-range profit has quite a different meaning to it than maximum profit. As business leaders look increasingly to the long-range survival and well-being of their companies, they inevitably will become more concerned with all of the environmental factors which will affect their future. As they do this, corporate philanthropic contributions are bound to become more significant.

I hear increasingly that the best young college graduates are not attracted to business. They are critical of business and businessmen for their standards and their motives. And they are sometimes right. Their intense desire to do something for society leads them to other professions and occupations.

If running a successful business isn't an effective way to serve society, American business will not attract the best young people. And how can it prosper if it can't attract them?

We in business must not be ashamed to say that our primary purpose is to serve society—our customers, our employees, our community—as well as our stockholders.

And if we are going to be really effective in this role, business must also take full advantage of the 5% tax deduction for charitable contributions. Corporations need then to vie for the most enlightened and effective use of this dollar, as they now do with their TV advertising dollar.

43

One corporation might want to concentrate on education, another on health and welfare programs, a third on the arts. Or corporations might want to divide their philanthropic dollars in many different ways among all the competing institutions.

However they decide to do it, it will require infinitely greater thought than is now exercised in many corporate giving programs. Creativity will be equally as important as control. Hopefully the day will come when corporations will be so proud of their giving programs that they will want to publicize their donations.

CORPORATIONS AND ART PARTICIPATION

The arts are an important factor in an area's economy. Relevant facts and figures which have been collected have, on more than one occasion, furnished helpful assistance to corporations seeking to expand in a given location or establish a new plant. Corporations are beginning to realize the importance of supporting activities in the arts on both a local and national basis, as a forward-looking policy of enlightened self-interest. They could well become tomorrow's most important arts patrons, supplying not only money, but also talented manpower and service.

In a recent statewide study, conducted by the Illinois Arts Council, in the areas of music, theater, visual arts and dance, and *not including* figures and facts in commercial theater, popular music, television and radio, it was found that millions of residents of Illinois, each year, attend arts programs, and spend over $70 million annually in the process. These arts activities provide well over 30,000 full-time jobs and a similar number of part-time jobs, and enlist the valuable talents of over 400,000 volunteers. These are conservative figures.

Corporate support of the arts, which is new money for the most part, will increase as the corporate managers are impressed with the management abilities of arts organizations, as well as their artistic offerings. The language of planning, research, market studies, cost analysis, and customer service applies here, and certainly is understood by the prospective corporate donor. He may have some difficulty in defining the arts and their role in our lives today, even though he may be increasingly aware of their importance, but he can certainly understand and recognize a well-administered arts organization. Only when the local arts organization has done the best job possible in managing itself, in setting artistic goals and

Extract of remarks by George M. Irwin, chairman, Quincy Compressor Division, Colt Industries, chairman, Illinois Arts Council, and chairman Associated Councils of the Arts, at various times and places

45

standards, in showing that it recognizes its total community role, can that group expect corporate officials to contribute corporate money, or the time and talents of company personnel.

Obviously, a first-class selling job is demanded when seeking corporate support for the arts. There is a growing recognition, however, on the part of corporate leaders that the corporation is truly a citizen of and has responsibilities to its community, as has the individual. Recognizing this responsibility, the corporate official will often want to know in what way his company will receive a return on the contribution. There are two types of dividends which can be pointed out: 1) the value of the programs of the arts organizations to the employees of the company, and 2) their actual participation in those programs, can be all that is needed to secure the contribution. In a long-range view, money spent on the public interest—which can often mean enlightened self-interest for the corporation—will provide a satisfying return.

Business for many years has handsomely supported health and welfare activities, and in the post-war period has become a significant source of financial support for our institutions of higher education. As these programs become stabilized and as departments of government increase their support of the health, welfare and education organizations, it is only natural that business should look to the field of the arts, a major area with which it has not yet been significantly concerned. The federal government has recognized the role of corporations as donors in these several fields by permitting corporations to deduct contributions of up to 5% of their pretax earnings.

I believe that more and more business leaders are recognizing that today's corporation has a social responsibility as well as an economic one. Its responsibility to make a profit continues to be as important as before, but its leaders realize that there are new ideals and responsibilities which go beyond the profit motive. This greater responsibility is, in effect, a recognition of the corporation's role as a full-fledged citizen of the community and the entire area which it serves. This is a natural evolution in the role of the corporation and not merely a change in its public relations image.

THE CORPORATION, THE ARTS AND THE GHETTO

Extract of remarks by C. Douglas Dillon, former Secretary of the Treasury, chairman, Business Committee for the Arts, before the Minnesota Orchestral Association, Minneapolis, June 27, 1968

The United States of America is the greatest and most powerful organization that the world has ever known. Yet, increasingly, here and abroad, there is recognition that even such a government as ours cannot solve all problems. It simply cannot heal all the ills of the world and is far from solving our own worst one, that one which has been troubling us for ten years and more, upsetting all the norms of our hard-earned civilization.

Now, this year, President Johnson has asked Henry Ford II to organize the nation's corporations to help. The people, the minorities as well as the majority, and the government itself most of all, are as a last resort—and it really is a last hope—looking to business to assist in solving our national crisis.

Elisha Gray, chairman of the board of the Whirlpool Corporation, recently stated this clearly: "We businessmen can put together more sheer power for good or for evil than all the rest of the elements of the community combined. Call it power—call it influence—call it clout. By any name, it is the ability to get things done."

And as the record is beginning to manifest, business is responding. The National Industrial Conference Board's studies show that never before has industry been so interested in socio-economic problems. Almost at once in this national crisis and upheaval, social problems have become business problems. Now the business of business *is* America.

Certainly, business attention is no longer focused solely on science, technology and finance. Management is now as deeply involved with our community and urban issues as any other institution or member of American society.

Executives of 1,000 companies recently surveyed by NICB say that they are willing to assume social responsibilities *in addition* to their traditional obligations of producing a product and giving a service of high quality to make a profit. Nearly nine out of ten of the firms that were surveyed urge their employees to volunteer time and effort to community groups of a social service, civic and cultural nature. In addition, corporate giving is estimated today at an all-time record of 750 million dollars.

It is encouraging to note that in the NICB survey I have mentioned, more than one-half the companies interviewed said that they would be willing to *initiate* action to solve civic problems, including the encouragement of more and better cultural facilities and activities.

Business is recognizing its obligations to society. Charles Lazarus, president both of the F & R Lazarus Company and the American Retail Federation, recently said: "The evidence is clear that business cannot prosper apart from the community in which it operates."

I am not suggesting that cultural programs should enjoy as high a priority as, for example, education for the disadvantaged. Nevertheless, it is significant that business is concerned with the arts and willing to stimulate their further development. The fact that artistic performances of one sort or another are essential in handling the crisis of our cities is too little realized. The lack of the cultural facilities for all the people is integral to the national crisis that is now gripping us. It has clear relevancy, particularly to the urban problems that we face.

One of the most effective ways the arts can be used is to provide a voice for the youth who live in the poverty areas. Through the mere act of communicating, they can achieve a power they did not have before. In fact, it is this ability to provide communication that makes the arts one of our most effective tools in the effort to rid our society of its most basic ills—voicelessness, isolation, depersonalization—the complete absence of any purpose or reason for living.

Business is beginning to see that it has the most to gain in maintaining culture

49

Above: Clairol, Inc.'s Teenage Leadership Program in cooperation with the New York City Dept. of Parks.

Below: Mobil Oil Corporation's five-borough ghetto area rock contest, "Operation Sound Search."

for and in the social structure in which it exists. Business is willing to take the initiative. The problem is that business has still to learn what needs exist. The ordinary businessman knows as little about the management and budgets of the arts as the arts now know about business.

Business needs the arts as a part of society, to attract industry, to create jobs and to recruit executives. The arts need business to support them morally as well as financially.

VALUE OF THE ARTS TO A CORPORATION

Extract of remarks by Leo H. Schoenhofen, chairman, Container Corporation of America, to New York businessmen at Lincoln Center, March 28, 1966

What are some of the forces from within which prompted us of the Container Corporation of America to take note of the whole man? First, if private enterprise is to be a major force in our society, then private industry has a responsibility to improve the quality of life here.

A second internal force includes the very human desire of employees to take pride in their jobs, and pride in the ability of their company to distinguish itself from all others.

Another much more subtle force was the result of the decline in the last century of the concept of "work as religion." As the idea waned that sheer production of goods was somehow almost holy, management began to cast about for a new justification for its labors. Management has begun to find this justification, I think, in responding to the new *need* to serve the public interest in areas beyond its traditional function of making and selling products. This is what has led to involvement with the customer as a total human being.

A business, after all, is *in* business. And the first responsibility—a moral responsibility, if you will permit me—is to remain that way, for the sake of its investors, its employees and its customers who presumably benefit from the association.

If pursuing that goal in an enlightened manner also results in an enrichment of the community, then that is a very happy coincidence of interest. But it is not the main objective of business. For the fact is, if more management groups practiced this kind of enlightened self-interest, we would have a much livelier, much more attractive cultural life in this country today.

My company's involvement in fine art revolves chiefly around the "Great

Ideas of Western Man" advertising series. This joining of fine art and philosophic statements is rooted deeply in business reality, the achievement of corporate goals. We understand and admire fine art and good design, but long ago we chose to identify ourselves with these elements, not chiefly for aesthetic reasons but for sound, strategic ones. The products of Container Corporation are essentially prosaic, but the design of these everyday items is of critical importance in the marketplace, and the pragmatic businessman understands this. A strong association of Container Corporation with fine art, good design, and great ideas helps us sell our product. It elevates our salesman in the eyes of people he calls upon. It predisposes at least some customers to do business with us.

We have also found that our particular approach has attracted some very high quality personnel.

Another benefit has been to create subtle but powerful discipline within the corporation, a kind of unofficial quality control mechanism. Whether we originally planned it or not, all our corporate activities began a long time ago to be measured against the "Great Ideas" level of quality and performance.

Somewhat narrower in scope, but influential nevertheless in encouraging a closer relationship between business and arts, is our use of prints and etchings as promotional material aimed at the business community. We also have established permanent art galleries in our corporate offices in New York and Chicago, devoted to an ever-changing series of one-man shows.

What does all this mean then—this picture of the big corporation commissioning the world's top artists to interpret a given concept, "programming" a whole cultural system, amassing a distinguished corporate collection of paintings and sculpture?

There is no doubt that some have viewed with alarm; have worried about the corruption of the artist in the executive suite; have wondered what will be

53

the dire results of the fact that an increasing percentage of private gallery sales are to the corporation, rather than to the individual or the museum. I would remind those who think such dark thoughts, that except for a relatively brief period in world history—the most recent period, in fact—the dominant center of power was always the major stimulus to art, serving as a sponsor and patron. It seems logical that the role of art patron should be assumed by this new major force in society, the corporate management team. There is nothing either new or sinister in the fact that they are using fine art for their own ends. That has almost always been true of art patrons. Industry must begin truly to believe in the arts, believe in them enough to use them selfishly, to put them to work for business rather than serving merely as corporate decoration.

CULTURAL ENVIRONMENT AIDS CORPORATIONS

The presence of cultural activities is a potent force in helping to make a city attractive to the new breed of college graduates and younger married people who have a strong social and cultural awareness. These are the people who challenge both the corporation and the community to utilize them and their talents completely. Increased productivity has provided us with increased leisure, and it is important to fill this time with rewarding experiences of the kind provided by many arts organizations.

The presence of a sound cultural environment was instrumental in attracting the Manned Spacecraft Center to Houston and will become increasingly more important in the future. The demands of our society are placing a strong burden on businessmen to become more fully aware individuals, and involvement with the arts can help add dimension and understanding to people. This melding of interests tends to enlarge the total man and make him more capable of solving the sophisticated new problems facing the corporation in a changing society.

The contributions of a thriving cultural life to business and to the community are therefore important and essential, and they must be continuously stressed. There is a responsibility on the part of the arts to merit and to seek recurring recognition for their contributions to the community and to do it in a compelling way.

Arts organizations must spell out their cases completely and compellingly. The corporation well recognizes its obligation to support important community and cultural activities, for corporate giving has deep roots in our social system. However, the company also has a responsibility to its shareholders to invest the corporate contribution where it will pay the greatest dividend to employees and to its environment.

Extract of remarks by Dr. Charles F. Jones, president, Humble Oil and Refining Company, before the Houston Chamber of Commerce, Houston, Texas, March 7, 1968

55

Business is required to run its own house effectively, and it expects evidence of the same approach in cultural organizations.

A potential corporate contributor wants to know the total current operating budget of an applicant arts organization as well as the estimated expenditures for the next year. To help us determine the general level of support for the organization by other firms in Houston, we ask for a list of major contributors.

We ask the question "What benefits do the community and the company derive from the work of this organization?" and complete our examination by trying to establish whether a lesser contribution would jeopardize these benefits.

Only after these and other similar questions are answered do we recommend support for an organization and assign a dollar figure. We give great weight to the program of work and to benefits derived by the city and the company.

There are four ways I feel in which the trend toward greater interaction between business and the arts could be heightened and in which communications between the two sectors could be strenghtened.

First, any cultural organization seeking major support from a specific company should carefully analyze the needs of the company and what makes it different from competing corporations.

After the basic personality of a particular company has been defined and its needs assessed, the second of the four points comes into play. In seeking major funds, be prepared to speak to the needs of the corporation and the community. There will be a person or committee within each company who will have to justify recommendations for contributions.

Third, continuous year-round communication of an appropriate nature will build greater awareness of arts programs for business. I feel it would be helpful to arrange selective appropriate contacts between cultural groups and business leaders throughout the year—perhaps in briefing sessions or through occasional letters bringing industrialists up to date on new developments.

The fourth method for building better interaction between the corporations and cultural groups is to consider the advantages of involving people from business on a volunteer basis. The benefits that can be derived from a substantial cash contribution are fairly obvious. Less specific, but perhaps more lasting, are the contributions that can be made by a committed and involved worker. I might point out that the same qualities which make a man valuable to us in business might be adapted to serve the needs of the cultural group and by extension the entire community.

We have found that one of the most effective ways to build understanding between businessmen and educators is to expose our bright and creative people periodically to the college environment through planned programs. In that way, we can help answer some of the questions being raised in the schools about individual achievement, personal convictions and stimulating work to be done in industry.

In the same way, I feel that greater personalized interchanges between the arts and industry would lead to greater understanding and a greater appreciation of each other's objectives. The cultural groups have, I feel, a rare opportunity to gain solid converts from business and at the same time profit by the analytical and organizational skills prized highly in industry. From his own point of view, the businessman might find a challenging new environment.

COMMERCE, INDUSTRY AND THE ARTS

Extract of remarks by Dr. Frank Stanton, president, Columbia Broadcasting System, Inc., before the Arts Council at Columbus, Ohio, February 23, 1967

Commerce, industry and the arts are, I think, on the eve of a new alliance everywhere in our country. This nation has been transformed in the past two decades. We are all becoming part of each other's world, and business is learning, along with every other sector of society, that it is not an island unto itself and that it both nourishes and is nourished by all those other activities that give any society character, richness, variety and meaning.

The purpose of liberal education is, basically, to enable us to make distinctions. The essence of successful business practice is to operate on distinctions. The arts carry distinctions to their logical, and very often their illogical, extremes. And so the first place to worry about American life losing its vital qualities of individualism is in the arts. If this happens, no liberal education will save our kind of society, and no business enterprise will long prosper in what is left of it.

There are many more immediate reasons why alert business managements are taking new and longer looks at the arts on local, regional and national scales:

To attract to a business career a fairer share of the brightest, most creative and most venturesome college students than the current 12 per cent who make it their first choice, business has got to offer a cultural environment as rich and varied and meaningful as that of competing fields;

To recruit able employees, plant communities must offer opportunities for employees and their families to make the most of their interests, their talents and their capacities;

To keep or to earn the respect of institutions, public and private, whose goodwill is necessary to vigorous business growth, a business must show regard for the

Artmobile donated by Dead River Company is used for Arts Showcase display.

Below, Bangor High School co-eds admire some sculpture.

standards of excellence, good taste and distinction that both inspire and are stimulated by the arts;

To understand the human context of a healthy business life, a continuing awareness of the arts is as essential to wise business leadership as it is to any other kind of leadership, spiritual, intellectual or social;

To make its way in an age and among a people increasingly tormented by conflicting demands upon its attention, business must constantly elevate the level of its communications style, design and fineness of substance.

I think that it is inevitable that the rise of business support of the arts will be no less dramatic than has been the case with education. This has been brought about by many factors—among them, modern communications; increased travel; the irrepressible growth in the number of museums and performing art centers; the rise of arts councils that channel, both outwardly and inwardly, activities in the arts; and the restless search, in an era of rapidly increasing leisure, for new meaning and new experience. All these factors are of mounting rather than declining force, that will create civic and social environments far more hospitable to the progress of business than narrow and deprived communities who hold out for the young—upon whom the growth of business as of everything else depends—only the hope of some day leaving them.

That is why it is not good enough to have only great national institutions of art. Business must be concerned that local and regional communities have lively art centers and activities of their own. It seems to me wholly relevant to the purpose of Chambers of Commerce to give them high priority in their long-range planning.

Art is not a remote thing, responsibility for which can be bucked over to some far center of funds or authority. It is the thing that preserves for all life—including business life and, perhaps, in a complex industrial society, especially business life—the human scale.

Business cannot always speak to individuals as individuals, and sometimes the new job that needs to be done, and the new capacities that we have to get it done, seem to fly in the face of human values. But business can still respect and prize the essential human core of all relationships both by going to school to the arts—all of them and however much they may occasionally jolt us—and by giving them all that they need from us: our sympathetic insight, our understanding and our material support.

The American of tomorrow is going to demand this of business anyhow. There is a new breed of American arising, and it is a breed in league with the arts. This coming generation is not going to be at home in an environment that says that the only concern of business is the 30-day balance sheet. They are going to relate the stewardship of business, as I believe they should, to a sharpened awareness of the environment in which it functions, a deepened sense of responsibility for the world towards which it moves, and a broadened vision of the forces that impel the total society forward.

This liberalizing of the liberally educated man, who will either go into business or have a determining effect upon the kind of world in which business makes its way, will inevitably be a powerful influence in shaping the character of the business management of the future. I believe that management is going to be more imaginative, more creative and more enterprising than anything we have seen in the past. Allied with this changing management is the professionalization of the business executive. In 1900, only 40 per cent of executives in big business had a higher education. By 1964, 90 per cent had, and among the younger executives 35 per cent also had had graduate study. Exposure to broader and longer educational experience, especially interdisciplinary curricula, is producing managements that see their missions—the furnishing of a product or a service—against a wider background than their own special business arenas and that find their fulfillment in larger terms than their own special business interests.

61

There is, in my opinion, no one question about which those now responsible for the economic prosperity of a community should be more seriously concerned, and on which it should be prepared to take more significant action, than whether the management of tomorrow is going to seek out the community or turn its back on it. Ours is an extremely mobile society. People and industries are both constantly on the move—seeking new opportunities in new places. (Last year one out of five families moved.) The competition for good enterprises and good people is strong. Better educated employees and managers, exposed to the arts in their youth as never before, are making tough demands of any community which they are considering as a possible home. The commercial and industrial community that does not realize this is just going to be out of the running.

PART THREE:
OPPORTUNITIES AND EXAMPLES

INTRODUCTION

Business involvement in community betterment should begin, like charity itself, at home. The businessman who has felt some stirring of the impulse to do something to help improve the quality of life in his community cannot do better than enlist the guidance of the local arts council, to learn of the opportunities to devote some of his money, and hopefully also some of his time, to the service of the arts. The arts are astir all over America. There is no better indication of this than that the number of community arts councils in the United States has increased well over a hundredfold in the postwar years—from 4 in 1946 to nearly 600 in 1968—and all of them are the conduits to the proliferating-like-mushrooms arts groups on the grass-roots or regional level.

Of the more than 4,200 museums of all kinds in this country, 620 are art museums. Since there are well over 15,000 cities and towns in this vast land, obviously only a relative handful have art museums of their own. To varying but similar degree, the same is true of all the other arts groups. Only some 15 of the 200 dance groups are established nonprofit professional companies; of the 1,450 orchestras, fewer than 1,000 are sufficiently professional to have membership in the American Symphony Orchestra League, but actually only about 80 are major or metropolitan orchestras deserving the "symphony" appellation in the commonly understood "full-dress" application of it; of the between 600 and 700 opera companies, only 35 to 40 perform professionally on anything like a regular basis; and of the approximately 5,000 theatrical groups, only 35 are resident professional theatres.

The businessman looking for deserving arts groups or ventures to help, and with which perhaps ultimately to become to some degree involved, will normally first look around locally. Either the local arts council or a nearby college should come up with some worthwhile suggestions.

Dr. Fannie Taylor, now coordinator of the University of Wisconsin Arts Council, says that "the college market today accounts for more than 70 per cent of the professional concert activity in the United States."

In all likelihood, between the arts council and the information office of the nearest college, the businessman with any inclination at all to take a first step towards corporate patronage of the arts will encounter an embarrassment of opportunities, with more than one deserving group activity or program literally crying out for support—and probably offering plenty of chance for involvement, too.

There are as many possible ways of contributing to these arts as the ingenuity of a businessman and the creative imagination of an artist (or *vice versa*) could conceive. Some of the multitudinous types of contributions are here considered in three principal categories: donation, participation and stimulation. This arbitrary division is not to establish felicity of phrase. It is to suggest the progress a corporation can make in its involvement in the arts and therefore in the society of its surroundings. Donation is good; participation is better; and stimulation is still better. Best, of course, for the executive minded of his corporation's involvement in the social structure, is all three.

A. DONATION

The Internal Revenue Service has since 1935 permitted deductions from corporate net income before taxes of up to five per cent for contributions to charitable, educational and cultural activities which have been established as tax-exempt. The Service defines (Sec. 170 (c) (2) (b)) a charitable contribution as one to "a corporation, trust, community chest, fund or foundation organized and operated exclusively for . . . literary, or educational purposes." Those organizations which are exempt from tax, and to whom corporate gifts may be tax-deductible, are (Sec. 501 (c) (3)): "Corporations, and any community chest, fund or foundation, organized and operated exclusively for . . . literary, or educational purposes, . . . no part of the net earnings of which inures to the benefit of any private shareholder or individual . . ."

Rabkin and Johnson, in their work, *Federal Income Gift and Estate Taxation,* explain the practical effect of these regulations for both corporations and recipient organizations:

"The Treasury's regulations and ruling policy are crucial for these organizations, not so much because of the tax exemption granted, but because of the deductibility of contributions. As a practical matter, it is virtually impossible to obtain public contributions for an organization which has not received its 'exemption certificate,' because no individual relishes the prospect of fighting for the charity's exemption in his own income tax examination. The Service, therefore, has life-or-death power over most charities in the exercise of its discretionary ruling policy."

This tends to explain the disinclination of corporations or their foundations to give to individuals or groups which have not established their tax-exempt status.

I am indebted to Joseph Taubman for the above material, taken from his review article, "Performing Arts—The Economic Dilemma," by Baumol & Bowen, appearing in *The Tulane Law Review* of December, 1968.

There are at least four ways in which a corporation may contribute to the various arts within the framework of the Internal Revenue Service stipulations. Obviously, contributions in this realm are best for the corporation. With corporate taxes hovering around fifty per cent, any gift is in effect matched by the Federal government. The four basic methods of donation discussed below are: cash contributions, direct subsidizing, indirect subsidizing and loans other than cash.

1. CASH CONTRIBUTIONS

This is for most the quickest and easiest method. It is also the least subject to challenge by the Internal Revenue Service. Bookkeeping is simplified, corporate costs for handling the gift are minimal. There is very little personal involvement required. The recipient organization is largely left to its own decision as to where the money will be best spent.

The four most usual types of such contributions are discussed below.

A. DIRECT GIFTS

These are the most frequent and bulk large in the National Industrial Conference Board estimate of corporate contributions to the arts. The company considers various criteria in selecting the recipient and writes a check. Hopefully it will receive some other notice of its impact on the arts group than the cancelled check, although all too often the artists, feeling as they frequently state that the corporation "has an obligation" to give them money, neglect to send even a courtesy letter of thanks. They forget or never knew that a direct gift can be a one-shot deal, and it is very likely to be so unless some effort is made to show how the money helped and to interest the donating executive in what they are doing.

The list of corporations giving in this manner is nearly as large as *Poor's Register of Corporations*. Almost every company makes some philanthropic donations during the year, although still far too few contribute to the arts.

B. MATCHING GIFTS

Under this plan the corporation matches, usually one to one, gifts by others to arts organizations. The other source could be anything from a government or foundation to an employee. The Council for Financial Aid to Education has been extremely successful in encouraging business support of educational institutions through this method.

Adolph's Food Products recently offered a challenge grant to the American Symphony Orchestra League, promising fifty cents for each "new" dollar the League raised.

Bristol-Myers contributed $300,000, which the National Endowment for the Arts matched with $325,000, to New York's Channel 13 educational television station. This permitted Channel 13 to produce 32 programs on its "Sunday Showcase" in the 1966-1967 period. These programs, varying in length from an hour to 90 minutes, included plays, musicals, puppetry and discussions of the fine arts. Channel 13 had never before been able financially to go on the air on Sunday with real productions.

C. SECURITIES

There are two basic types of gifts of securities which a corporation might want to consider. In the case of direct gifts, there is a tax deduction available for the market value of the securities as of the date of the gift, and there is no capital

69

gains tax on the increased value. Out-of-pocket cost for the corporation is reduced by the resulting tax benefits.

In the case of donative sale, securities which have greatly increased in value may be sold to an arts group at their original cost. The difference between the original cost and the current market value is a tax-deductible contribution. Under this arrangement, the corporation recovers its original investment and receives a tax deduction for the gift.

D. UNITED ARTS FUNDS

Some eighteen cities of the United States currently have united arts fund drives, similar to community fund drives. A corporate gift to such a fund would usually be divided among the arts groups as predetermined by the fund's board. The advantage to the corporation is of course that this method obviates the necessity of examining and evaluating the recipient arts groups.

Michael Newton, executive director of The Arts and Education Council of Greater St. Louis, discussed some of the problems of his extremely successful united art fund drives in *Cultural Affairs,* the magazine of the Associated Councils of the Arts. He felt that while the annual drive had increased the level of giving by 50 per cent from 1965 to 1968, some worthwhile new organizations in the area which had not been able to participate in the united fund could not get the support they needed. Nevertheless, such united drives, largely organized by the business community through an elite corporate leadership, have frequently been found the best method of obtaining corporate fiscal support of the local arts groups.

E. GOODS

The practice of giving goods to an arts group is widespread. Frequently such a gift can be more valuable to the recipient than actual money, for the company

Vermont Marble Company co-sponsored Vermont International Sculptors Symposium in Proctor, Vermont, 1968.

can donate something which would cost the arts organization much more than the real value on the open market—secondhand or obsolescent equipment, for example.

Columbia Broadcasting System regularly offers nonprofit television stations used but still highly serviceable studio and other equipment gratis when it buys new materials for its own use. In 1960, the Ampex Corporation gave National Educational Television in New York $311,000 worth of equipment and the 3M Corporation $252,000 worth of videotape.

General Electric recently gave the City Center Joffrey Ballet equipment with which to record its performances. All ballet companies have extreme difficulty in recalling, after a passage of time, exactly how the dancing was performed. There is no way of writing it down in words or scoring it musically. Diagrams have proved less than adequate. Film is the only practicable method, and this current GE gift helps the Joffrey Ballet alleviate a mind-splitting difficulty.

A number of corporations donate goods they do not themselves produce, some on the logical assumption that they can get the goods wholesale or at least at a cost less than the arts organization would have to pay. Kansas Gas & Electric Company, of Wichita, is on *Esquire*'s "Honor Roll" of business supporters of the arts for having donated a tractor-van when it sponsored an Artmobile tour by the Wichita Art Museum.

Some corporations contribute works of art which they purchase. Sears-Roebuck Foundation provides contemporary paintings to the Southern Arts Festival for permanent collections. The Container Corporation of America has given original art to museums and galleries in Chattanooga, Cincinnati, New York, Chicago, and Knoxville. Rich's Department Store in Atlanta received an *Esquire* award for, among other things, giving a 22-foot bronze sculpture to the City of Atlanta.

This type of donation, however, brings frequent questioning by the Internal

Stokely-Van Camp, Inc., The Indianapolis Power & Light Co., Burger Chef Systems, Inc. and The Indianapolis Foundation joined to bring Twilight Concerts in the Park to Indianapolis, Indiana in 1968.

Revenue Service when a corporation attempts to deduct the value as a philanthropic contribution. The deduction allowed is the "fair market value," and in determining this all relevant factors must be considered. This would include the cost or selling price, sales of similar items, cost of replacement and even opinion evidence and appraisals.

2. DIRECT SUBSIDIZING

Direct subsidizing also usually involves the contribution of cash by the corporation, but there is a significant difference. The money is given for a specific and limited purpose to the art organization, in return for the organization's performing specified acts. Such an operation is, in the usual case, a purchase of services, and the corporation negotiates the deal for its own reasons.

This does not mean that direct subsidizing does not help the arts group recipient. In fact, it invariably does help measurably. The company, however, in these instances can and does claim to aid its corporate image as well as perform philanthropic good for the arts and the society of which both are a part.

An advantage to the arts groups of this kind of support is that it usually involves corporate participation at the executive, employee or customer level—or all three. Thus the arts can anticipate stimulation of interest and perhaps further subsidizing and participation.

An advantage to the corporation is that such direct subsidizing can frequently be tied in with advertising, public relations, etc., and provide a direct rebuttal to any stockholder objections.

A. PURCHASE OF TICKETS

74

This can be done directly or indirectly. Basically, the concept is that a corporation buys tickets to performances or pays a portion of the price of tickets for arts presentations, the remainder being paid by the purchaser of the tickets.

The Archer-Daniels-Midland Company subsidizes a fixed amount of the purchase price of Minneapolis Symphony Orchestra tickets: the employee pays the balance.

Members of the Postal Workers Union present coupons and a dollar sum at the box office of the New York Philharmonic, to buy available tickets. At the end of the month, the New York Philharmonic totes up the coupons and sends them to the Postal Workers Union for reimbursement.

Similarly, the Alley Theatre, in Houston, recently initiated a variation with its "Corporate Coupon" program. Seven young local bank executives there volunteered to personally encourage corporations of the area to buy books of coupons which their employees might redeem at the box office for tickets.

Many companies purchase boxes at the opera or blocks of seats at plays regularly for various business guests. They write these off in their entertainment expense budget.

The newly-organized Theatre Development Fund encourages the presentation of new and better plays on Broadway through subsidizing tickets during the perilous first weeks of a production. If the play is successful, the producers will repay the Theatre Development Fund from its profits. The first such subsidized plays were *Great White Hope* and *We Bombed in New Haven*. A corporate gift to this organization would in a sense come under this category of subsidizing.

Neiman-Marcus of Dallas received an *Esquire* award for its "catalytic" impact on the cultural life of its community. Involved here were the department store's efforts to bring the best of the world's arts and artists to Dallas for performances at which the price of tickets was within the reach of all.

Rheingold Breweries of Brooklyn received an *Esquire* award for developing

75

and sponsoring the Central Park Music Festival, a summer-long music series present-ing the full spectrum of popular entertainment—classical guitar, Spanish dance, music of other nations, jazz and rhythm and blues—for the low admission fee of $1.00 per performance.

B. SUBSIDIZING PRESENTATIONS

A recent study by Management Survey and Search Corporation, consultants, revealed that middle and top management executives working in California, New York or New England will tend to resist invitations to relocate. Contrariwise, the most mobile executives are in the Midwest, South, Middle Atlantic States and the Northwest.

Corporations of national stature have recognized this fact of executive life for some time. To resist the trend, and to attract and keep executives of high caliber in less culturally active areas of the country, they paraphrase Mohammed and bring the culture to the executive before he reverses the process.

Alvin H. Reiss wrote in *Arts Management,* September-October, 1967 of a corpo-rate subsidy of a ballet tour. Three businessmen helped spearhead a drive to bring the City Center Joffrey Ballet to the Pacific Northwest for a two-month program which included a one-month residency with rehearsals and workshops at Pacific Lutheran University in Tacoma, a performing tour of five cities in the states of Washington and Idaho, and a six-week scholarship project in which talented dance students from four Pacific Northwest states studied with the company. Goodwin Chase, president of Tacoma's National Bank of Washington, Claude Blair of Seattle's Northwest Bell Telephone Company, and Robert Hansberger, president of Boise Cascade Corporation in Idaho, joined to establish the Pacific Northwest Ballet Association to sponsor the program.

An all-out fund-raising drive by the Ballet Association resulted in more than

City Center Joffrey Ballet rehearsals at Pacific Lutheran University, Tacoma, Washington. The residency was co-sponsored by Boise Cascade Corporation, National Bank of Washington and Northwest Bell Telephone Company executives.

500 contributions from corporations and individuals in Washington and Idaho, including major grants from the city of Tacoma and from PONCHO, a cultural organization in Seattle.

Alexander Ewing, the Ballet's general director, reports that the program was as successful in the summer of 1968 as it was in 1967, and it will be repeated in 1969. He adds that the Joffrey Ballet has itself received many unexpected dividends from this activity. In the autumn of 1968 when a principal dancer became indisposed, a young girl from Seattle took over the part beautifully. She had been a student at the Company's residency and workshop there.

The Toledo Edison Company received an *Esquire* award in 1967 for sponsoring the annual "Music Under the Stars" series of free classical and light-classical concerts in the Toledo Zoo Amphitheater. Comprising eight Sunday night concerts in July and August by the Toledo Concert Band, the series is attended by over 30,000 persons each session and is heard on radio by additional thousands of residents.

The Air Preheater Company, in Wellsville, New York was added to *Esquire*'s "Honor Roll" for initiating and underwriting a five-performance season of performing arts, including additional in-class high school performances, in a community otherwise totally deprived of such attractions.

Capitol Broadcasting Company, Raleigh, North Carolina received an *Esquire* award for sponsoring tours by the Metropolitan Opera National Company. Sixty-six performances were presented in 1967. Among them were 25 in North Carolina schools; these were preceded by a study of materials provided by the broadcasting company.

Columbia Gas of Pennsylvania has for some fifteen years sponsored concerts by the Pittsburgh Symphony Orchestra in small, neighboring communities that could not, on their own, support the appearance of a full symphony orchestra.

Samuel C. Johnson on wooden settee created by Wendell Castle (l.) and selected for inclusion in "OBJECTS: USA, The Johnson Collection of Contemporary Crafts," a travelling exhibition assembled by the Johnson Wax Company, Racine, Wisconsin.

The Columbus National Bank of Providence, R. I. sponsors an annual series of tour performances of the Rhode Island Philharmonic Orchestra. Known as Family Concerts, because the tickets are low-priced, these tours bring the orchestra to many communities not otherwise reached for economic reasons.

International Business Machines has long recognized the need for keeping its executives in Armonk, New York. As early as 1939 it wisely established a Department of Arts and Science to develop and coordinate extensive programs in support of the fine arts.

The Mead Corporation's "Art Across America" exhibit was conceived and put together by Arthur L. Harris, president of Scripto, Inc., formerly vice-president of The Mead Corporation. Originally a small regional competition to select a "Painting of the Year" which Harris purchased himself, it grew to be a major exhibition of 50 works of art drawn from all over the United States and shown as widely. Frequently the paintings were shown in museums, but, as Harris says, "We feel art is for the people. And we've found that many people in this country have not learned to go to their museums and feel comfortable about it." So they were as often shown in other exhibit areas. He feels that the Mead exhibit contributes to society in two unassuming ways: "We may have accelerated the recognition of an artist or two" and are "bringing to the public a cross-section of what the artists in America are doing."

C. COMMISSIONING OF WORKS

There is a trend, largely in New York City, towards this type of corporate involvement in the arts. The arts organization determines what new production it needs, budgets out the cost, and the corporation is invited to purchase the package. The contributions of Eastern Air Lines and American Export and Isbrandtsen Lines to the Metropolitan Opera have already been mentioned. Larry Aldrich Associates, of New York, contributed in a slightly different way to win a

New York Board of Trade award in 1966 "for the encouragement of young and unknown artists through special corporate commissions to selected artists and through annual purchase grants to the Museum of Modern Art and the Whitney Museum of American Art."

When the City Center Joffrey Ballet wanted to produce the new and psychedelic "Astarte," which made the cover of TIME magazine, they approached the Overseas National Airways for commissioning of the production. As Alex Ewing, the Ballet's manager, says: "They behaved so handsomely they took all the torture out of it. In a couple of days after the request, although they knew nothing about 'Astarte' they came back with a simple 'O.K.'" The Ballet's program carries a brief note to the effect that the *stockholders* of Overseas National Airways made the contribution.

3. INDIRECT SUBSIDIZING

The corporation involved in this method usually has no control over the activities of the artistic group subsidized. Cooperation is offered to help publicize the activity, but money, if given, is given indirectly and with no strings.

A. NEWSPAPER ADVERTISEMENTS

Macy's and Abraham and Straus in New York have been leaders in placing newspaper advertisements for arts activities as a public service. A typical Abraham and Straus ad in the September 9, 1968 *New York Times* in a seven-column spread mentions Abraham & Straus once besides the "salute:"

A & S salutes THE FIRST GREAT "FESTIVAL OF DANCE" SUB-SCRIPTION SEASON AT THE BROOKLYN ACADEMY OF MUSIC ... WITH 9 SERIES BY 9 SUPERB AMERICAN COMPANIES.

81

The ad includes a coupon to be sent to the Brooklyn Academy of Music requesting further information.

David Yunich, president of Macy's told why a department store should get involved in such activity.

Macy's runs in the New York newspapers over 100 "salute" ads a year. They have welcomed to New York, on the part of Macy's and all New Yorkers, everything from individual visiting artists like Marcel Marceau to the Metropolitan Opera's national company.

These ads stem from a very basic philosophy that what's good for New York is good for Macy's. Anything that makes the city more exciting, a more desirable place in which to live or work or visit, is bound to help Macy's because it will bring more people to the city. Macy's feels it a civic responsibility to encourage and publicize the arts in each community as much as it is its responsibility to promote good roads and clean air.

The effect on the arts of the Macy "Salute" is even greater than it is on the Macy image. The ads are virtually a Macy endorsement. Macy's files are filled with letters that tell of houses sold out, of hundreds of tickets bought, of tremendous interest evoked, as a direct result of the Macy ads.

This goes beyond the giving of monies or time or personal help because it brings others—the general public—into the involvement. A large retail establishment that reaches a vast number of people immediately and intimately is not the only kind of business that can involve the general public. Any corporation whose product or service is aimed at the consumer can do the same thing.

The arts cannot exist in a vacuum, even in a solid-gold-lined-vacuum—with the gold provided by corporations or government agencies. A singer does not sing for himself. A symphony orchestra does not play for a few enthusiasts. A dancer does not perform before an empty auditorium. A painter or sculptor does not create solely for his own pleasure. At least—not for long.

For the arts to survive today, the base of public interest and public support must be constantly broadened. It is the responsibility of corporations who reach this public day after day to turn it into an audience for these arts. Or, to put it another way, to expose the arts and the public to each other. When this has been done, the results are always gratifying. People today want to participate in the arts. Business must show them how and when and where. They no longer have to be told why.

Stix, Baer and Fuller of St. Louis received an *Esquire* award for, among other good works, the donation of full-page newspaper advertisements saluting cultural institutions.

Foley's of Houston received an *Esquire* commendation partly for contribution of free advertising to cultural activities in the community. The Home Savings and Loan Association of Rockford, Illinois also gives free newspaper advertising, and the Jefferson Standard Broadcasting Company, of Charlotte, North Carolina received an *Esquire* accolade in part for its publication of a cultural events calendar.

B. ELECTRONIC MEDIA SPONSORSHIP

The most outstanding and longstanding example of corporate sponsorship of the arts in radio is the 25-year-old Texaco "Metropolitan Opera of the Air." Their *Esquire* award cited Texaco for its sponsorship of Saturday afternoon opera broadcasts which reach an estimated 2,000,000 radio listeners per broadcast in communities throughout the country, comprising the largest opera audience in history. This project has been called "the greatest single contribution to the musical culture of the United States."

King Sooper's of Denver sponsors Denver radio broadcasts of leading symphony concerts.

The Hawaiian Electric Company of Honolulu promotes young musicians in radio broadcasts.

In television, WBZ-TV, the Westinghouse Broadcasting Company, Boston created and conducts The National Instrumentalist Competition—open to performers of the piano, violin, viola and cello—to enable "the most gifted young solo artist in the United States" to embark on a professional career.

The Illinois Bell Telephone Company received an *Esquire* award for underwriting a full year's showing of the "Chicago Festival" series of weekly television programs featuring the cultural activities of the Chicago area, including the Chicago Lyric Opera, the Ravinia Summer Music Festival, and the Chicago Art Institute's Matisse exhibit.

C. ADVERTISEMENTS IN PROGRAMS

Another means of indirect subsidizing is through the placement of corporate advertisements in programs of performing arts and fine arts organizations. This practice is so widespread as to require little elaboration. Usually the arts organization tries only, through the selling of such ads, to pay for the printing of the programs. Little is ever left over for activity.

An advantage of this method, however, is that the corporation can usually take such money from its advertising budget, and therefore it is more easily accessible on short notice.

D. CONTRIBUTIONS THROUGH EMPLOYEES

The *Reader's Digest* has established a unique new way of corporate giving, different from the "matching fund" concept and yet embodying some of those principles. The method is quite simple. The corporation has set aside a sizeable sum for a carefully selected group of its employees, divided the money according to their rank and related factors, and allowed them to give their share to nonprofit organizations they select themselves.

Not all of the magazine's employees participate in the program. In 1965, some 690 did so. In 1966 the figure was 750—approximately one-third of the magazine's total work force.

The magazine's decision on who may participate is based on evaluation of how well a given employee shoulders responsibility, regardless of his rank or income. It is made solely on an employee's approach to his job. They do not check whether an employee is active in civic work.

The *Digest* makes no internal announcement of who may participate and who may not. It writes to the chosen employee at his home, including with the letter an application blank on which he can list the organizations he wants to give to.

Each employee may give his money to a single organization or divide it among several. He lists his choices on the application blank, then returns the blank to the treasurer's office. Roughly a week later, he receives his check or checks, made out to the organizations of his choice. He may send the checks out in any fashion he chooses.

4. LOANS (OTHER THAN FISCAL)

Often times the loan by a corporation of some of its facilities can be of measurably more help to an arts organization than the gift of money. It is not always, however, a tax-deductible item for presentation to the Internal Revenue Service. Although statistics to prove the prevalence of such loans are sadly lacking, there does seem to be a groundswell of such activity by corporations.

A. PERSONNEL

"Lending executives increases as do-good groups, politicians seek help," remarked *The Wall Street Journal* in a short article in its September 3, 1968 issue.

85

The article concludes: "An outside assignment 'helped me get promoted faster than I might have been otherwise,' claims an oil-company personnel man."

In order to further this activity, the Business Committee for the Arts is establishing a "Business-Arts Advisory Corps" composed of volunteer corporate executives willing to lend their services in such practical business methods as accounting and inventory, engineering, fund raising, and development. Such help will be primarily on a local basis for varying periods as necessary.

B. SPACE

Auditoriums

It is an interesting sidelight here that all new office buildings in Tokyo are required to include an auditorium for cultural performances. David Yunich, president of Macy's, asserts that each new Macy store includes an auditorium for events, courses, concerts, plays, or any activity that needs a hall or an arena. The range is from practical lectures on how to invest in stocks to serious drama. The desire to share in these activities is so great that the auditoriums bulge with interested participants, and tickets are issued, well in advance, on a strictly first-come, first-served basis.

Brentano's in New York received an award from the New York Board of Trade "for sponsoring 'Tonight at Eight,' a series of free programs of the fine and performing arts presented in their Fifth Avenue store."

The Rouse Company, of Baltimore, received an *Esquire* award for sponsoring and providing facilities for a continuing series of artistic performances, exhibits and other activities in nine communities in Kentucky, Maryland, New Jersey, Ohio, Pennsylvania and Texas. Exhibitions of sculpture, etchings, lithographs and woodcuts, as well as performances of opera, classical music and drama, are among the events.

86

Exhibits

Many companies include space for exhibits of various types in their buildings. Sometimes this is a simple window display of the works of local artists; often, as in many corporate headquarters on Park Avenue, it is an entire ground floor.

Hallmark Cards received one of the first "Business and the Arts" awards from the New York Board of Trade "for sponsoring five Hallmark Art Award competitions at the Hallmark Gallery on Fifth Avenue."

The Hoffman Fuel Company of Danbury, Connecticut operates an on-premise art gallery.

The Fayette Bank and Trust Company of Uniontown, Pennsylvania received an *Esquire* award for establishing an art exhibit on bank premises, the first of its kind in the community.

The Honolulu Advertiser received an *Esquire* award for its support of young local artists and for its on-premise gallery, the Contemporary Arts Center of Hawaii, which mounted 13 exhibits in 1967 ranging from the very modern to the very traditional.

Ticket Sales

Providing space on company premises for the sale of tickets to performing arts activities seems to be limited to department stores. Foley's of Houston is listed on *Esquire*'s "Honor Roll" for, among other aids to the arts, providing free ticket-selling facilities.

David Yunich said that in its first two years of this activity Macy's sold over a million dollars worth of theater tickets. A recent survey, comparing people who bought tickets at Macy's with those who went to the theaters to buy them, found that three times as many people at the Macy's box office had not been to a

87

Broadway show in over a year. These were clearly new customers for Broadway and very important for the theater industry.

Macy's maintains the box office, Yunich said, partly because they believe that the theater will only flourish if everyone supports it in every way he can, and partly because the theater is an attraction that brings many people into the city, and many of them end up spending money at Macy's. They do it, too, because making the arts available is a service to today's customer.

Macy's civic responsibility is double-barrelled. "We have a responsibility to the arts—to promote and promulgate, to support and foster them. At the same time, we have a responsibility to our customers—to the people in the communities we serve—to inform them, to educate them, to stimulate their interest, and yes, even to lead them to the satisfactions and pleasures inherent in the arts."

C. EQUIPMENT

The sharing of corporate equipment with various arts groups is becoming prevalent as executives begin to recognize the possible advantages to the company. Dr. Frank Stanton was as usual ahead of the general corporate community when in 1967 he urged business to finance annual "residencies" by artists in laboratories and other facilities where they could gain firsthand knowledge of new materials, techniques and technologies. He then announced that the CBS Foundation would provide funds for two such residencies, one for a painter and one for a sculptor, during the next year. "The artist needs," he said, "to get out of the eight-hour stint in the studio and become acquainted with the laboratory, the foundry, the plastics shop, the factory. Obviously, the artist cannot create his own complex for this. He must depend on industry."

Stanton expressed the hope that other corporations would join in this type of enterprise, considering it an imaginative and practical support of the arts.

Very possibly in answer to Stanton's example and exhortation, 20 technological and industrial corporations a year later joined with the Los Angeles County Museum of Art in a program to establish new art forms in new media, according to *The New York Times* on October 22, 1968. In the first phase, artists will work in residence in a corporation for three months, creating new forms of art using available materials and technologies. The second phase, of course, will be an exhibition at the Museum in 1970.

"Patron Sponsors," each of whom has agreed to take an artist in residence and also contributed $7,000 to the Museum, include the American Cement Corporation, Ampex Corporation, Litton Industries, International Business Machines Corporation, Universal City Studios Corporation and Lockheed Aircraft Corporation. Other organizations, offering to take an artist in residence but contributing less money, are the Philco-Ford Corporation, Newlett-Packard Company and Rand Corporation. Companies making smaller contributions but still actively involved in the project are Twentieth Century-Fox Film Corporation, Bank of America and North American Rockwell Corporation.

Perhaps the best and most widely coordinated joint activity of science and the arts is the Experiment in Arts and Technology. Begun in 1967 to bring artists and engineers together in practical, working collaboration, in mid-1968 it held its first international conference and announced chapters as far from its New York origin as Vancouver, British Columbia, and Sao Paulo, Brazil. *The National Observer,* in a July 22, 1968 article, noted that the Experiment in Arts and Technology (EAT) appeals to all kinds of people not usually involved with art or artists. Its several administrative committees include politicians (Senator Jacob Javits among them), scientists, architects and businessmen. EAT has also allied itself with organized labor on several levels. Theodore W. Kheel, the labor mediator, is chairman of EAT's executive committee. His support, and that of Harry Van Arsdale,

89

Jr., president of the AFL-CIO's Central Labor Council in New York City, have brought concrete results in the labor movement for EAT.

Corporations supporting the Experiment in Arts and Technology include American Telephone and Telegraph Company, International Business Machines Corporation, Bell Telephone Company, Xerox Corporation and the Edmund Scientific Company. Other corporate supporting members are the Essex Wire Company, Atlantic Richfield Corporation, Automatic Sprinkler Corporation, Broadway Maintenance Company, E. A. Kahn and Company, Schweber Electronics, Perfect Film Corporation and Martin E. Segal and Company.

5. COMMUNITY IMPROVEMENT

A. COMMUNITY ARTS CENTERS

Hundreds of community arts centers are being planned or built around the country, for various reasons including strong chauvinism which raises the cry, "We're cultured, too." Alvin H. Reiss, in the Spring, 1968, *The Drama Review,* discusses the matter in detail in his article, "Who Builds Theatres and Why?" According to Reiss, chauvinism is far from the sole motive for building a center. Many local businessmen are beginning to see culture as a commodity, one which brings in tourist dollars and helps local industry. He found that while over-all corporate support for the performing arts remains low, there has been strong business support for new cultural facilities. Reiss believes such support for the centers is influenced by the aforementioned "edifice complex." Gifts for a structure are relatively easy to come by, but continuing support of the activities housed in the center is lacking.

The Kennedy Center in Washington, D. C. raised $6 million from corporations, and the Lincoln Center $10.1 million. Chambers of commerce have played key roles in motivating and planning new arts facilities. Examples are those in Lewiston,

90

Idaho; Annapolis, Maryland; Charleston, South Carolina; Baton Rouge, Louisiana; San Jose, California; Evansville, Indiana; Winter Garden, Florida and Columbus, Ohio. The attitude of industry was summed up in a report to the Columbus Chamber of Commerce's Cultural Affairs Committee: "There is little question that an aggressive cultural program in Columbus can pay dividends to the business community, and that, if wisely planned, a cultural center can help implement such a program.'"

Goodyear Tire and Rubber Company gave $1,250,000 to the University of Akron Center for the Performing Arts, to tie the university area into the downtown business section.

B. ARTS IN THE GHETTO

Neil H. Anderson, executive vice president of the New York Board of Trade, commented in the March-April, 1968 *Arts Management* on the activities of New York's local arts councils to foster community understanding. In each of the five boroughs there are conglomerate populations, a wide divergence of economic levels and a whole spectrum of educational and social extremes. Yet each arts council in each of the boroughs reports the same story. Citizens of each community, rich and poor, white and black and Puerto Rican, have been busy working together peacefully and enthusiastically with the single objective of promoting the arts. Perhaps the most important aspect of this involvement with the arts has been the extraordinary dialogue that has been established. Without the self-consciousness of programs carefully structured to promote integration, the arts provide the opportunity for individual contact among people from all walks of life sharing a common goal.

The Sears-Roebuck Foundation of Skokie, Illinois gives scholarships to permit Watts students to attend the Idyllwild School of Music and Art.

P. Ballantine and Sons of Newark received an *Esquire* award for sponsoring

91

the "Jazzmobile" programs which included more than 50 free concerts in ghetto streets and under-privileged neighborhoods of New York City, Westchester County, Hartford, New Haven, Bridgeport, Philadelphia and Washington, D. C.

Mobil Oil Corporation of New York was also cited by *Esquire* for its sponsorship of "Operation Sound Search," a five-borough ghetto area rock contest culminating in a "finals" concert in Central Park, New York City.

The annual Cleveland Summer Arts Festival was first made possible in 1967, according to Dr. Leonard A. Glick, president of the Board of Trustees, by "the extraordinary fund-raising performance of Group 66, an organization of young business executives interested in civic affairs."

Although Cleveland had some difficulties in 1968, the second year of the Festival, the 1967 Festival was considered highly successful in instilling new vigor in the neighborhoods and adding new dimensions to the lives of thousands of inner city residents. The project brought Cleveland's outstanding cultural resources to its people. For example, in 68 days 153,165 children and adults attended 103 free performances by noted performing artists of Shakespeare, comic opera, ballet, modern dance and popular-type entertainment.

Probably the most dramatic activity was the series of free cultural arts workshops for children and adults in art, drama, dance and music, conducted at 14 neighborhood centers and schools, The Cleveland Play House, The Cleveland Museum of Art and Karamu House. Total attendance was 44,582. In the later weeks of the Festival children from the workshops performed to standing-room audiences at neighborhood centers.

According to Howard Whittaker, director of the Festival, the program also, among many other benefits, demonstrated a massive interracial effort by groups of varying backgrounds and walks of life working toward a common goal; developed neighborhood arts committees in conjunction with settlements to serve as local coordinating groups for neighborhood programs; employed more than 200 teenagers to assist in workshops and for other Festival-connected duties; and involved the Welfare Federation, particularly the Neighborhood Centers Association which includes most of the neighborhood centers throughout the city.

Whittaker concludes that in the summer of 1967 "Cleveland was a swinging city, with thousands of Clevelanders enjoying the summer months, attending programs with new friends and neighbors, and being exposed to new cultural interests."

C. IMPROVEMENT OF PHYSICAL ENVIRONMENT

Many communities, especially industrial ones in the East, have become run-down from their heyday in the early nineteen hundreds. Houses that were then splendors of monstrosity have been allowed to deteriorate as their original owners left them and as taxes were prohibitively increased. Many became slums, and inexorably taxes were increased in other areas of the city to compensate for the lack of income there. This action and consequent reaction, leading to the rapid abandonment of whole cities, could be halted and reversed, thoughtful citizens decided, through restoration of buildings and general improvement of the areas. An early and prime example is Georgetown in the District of Columbia. From a hot, humid slum it has been brought to a well kept, air conditioned upper suburbia.

In Columbus, Indiana the Cummins Engine Foundation has found a way to rejuvenate the city. It pays the fees of top architects to design the best of modern buildings. Architects who have been involved in the project include Eliel and Eero Saarinen, I. M. Pei, Eliot Noyes and Associates, Harry Weese and John Carl Warnecke. Even the Federal government cooperated when a new post office was to be installed there. When the rows of ornate late nineteenth century buildings on the main street were to be restored, Alexander Girard was the color consultant. And Robert Trent Jones designed the community golf course. J. Irwin Miller, presi-

93

Paley Park, on East 53rd Street, contributed by the William S. Paley Foundation as an oasis in New York.

dent of the Foundation, puts his argument succinctly: "Mediocre buildings have short lives. It's expensive to be mediocre."

The William S. Paley Foundation received a 1968 New York State award for Paley Park, situated on 53rd Street in New York between Madison and Fifth Avenues, two of the busiest and noisiest thoroughfares in the world. The citation was for providing a model and an incentive for the construction of small-site parks in congested urban areas. Paley Park is boxed in by tall buildings, and it occupies only 42 feet of frontage on a typical midtown side street. Despite these disadvantages, it provides a relaxing atmosphere, manages somehow to convey an impression of spaciousness, and with the restful, natural sound of its visually pleasing "waterfall" muffles the incessant city din.

B. PARTICIPATION

Participation in arts activities can be a rewarding experience for any executive willing to try it. It can also be rewarding for the arts organization or group with which he associates, for the adage about charity's commencing where the heart is applies as well to the arts as to the home. A person who works with, suffers for and participates in any group, performing or fine arts, finds that the money he gives in addition is no longer a charitable contribution but has become a gift of love, true philanthropy.

John J. O'Connor, in a *Wall Street Journal* article of October 14, 1968 finds in Cincinnati, as a result of the education boom of the past two decades, an increasing awareness of the quality of life, a new concern for the cultural environment or simply recreation. The young executive, O'Connor says, is no longer merely the savant in accounting or chemistry; he is likely to be more concerned with education and social problems in his community and about good theater and good food. Businesses are finding that an attractive salary is no longer always enough to attract top talent to the Midwest.

So O'Connor finds the corporation taking an active interest in Cincinnati cultural affairs. He sees no startling transformation; in fact, he says, there has too often only been startled confusion. But changes, however subtle, are being effected.

After a discussion of the cultural activities of Cincinnati on many levels, O'Connor concludes that "large parts of Cincinnati emerge now as anything but dowdy. Things are happening and there are enough participatory types around to see that they continue to happen. There still can be found the good burgher satisfied with the status quo, and the young couple who think about retiring to Europe in a few years to get away from the provincialism of it all. But the others seem increasingly to be at the controls."

Note what our English friends would call the operative word in the last paragraph, "participatory." These are the people who are revitalizing Cincinnati. Undoubtedly some of them are the young executives, people who become involved and through that involvement help their city and their society.

The four types of participation considered here for corporate executives represent increasing degrees of personal involvement: attendance at performances, management activities, participation in actual productions and organization of an arts group.

1. ATTENDANCE AT PERFORMANCES

This is the *sine qua non* of any involvement in the arts. It is not enough to purchase tickets to the opera. The empty seats of the patrons who give without participating echo hollowly to the singer and throw him off balance. Little can be more pleasing to actor or dancer than a full house in front of him. A rapport is established across the proscenium, and more enjoyment is had on both sides of it.

The theater, the concert hall, the museum and the library cannot long exist, no matter how great their financial backing, without an audience. They atrophy and die for lack of participation by the society for which they were, after all, created.

The audience does not, except in an indirect sense, control the trend of the theater or museum. Certainly, if no one comes to see an experimental exhibit or play that particular type will not be repeated without some thought. In the end it is the count at the turnstile that determines whether or not a city's cultural activities shall expand or decrease.

97

One of every three persons in the La Crosse Community Theatre production of "Guys and Dolls" was affiliated with The Trane Company, La Crosse, Wisconsin.

2. MANAGEMENT ACTIVITIES

Management assistance can be a great boon to an arts organization. One need not be chairman of the opera board to influence the course of the arts. One can serve in many other advisory capacities. David Yunich emphasizes the importance Macy's places on the involvement of its executives not only with the welfare of the store but also with the communities of which they and Macy's are a part. Such executives are, he says, better merchants and better people, with more perspective and more understanding because of the time and effort spent in such activities. "We want the men and women working for us to grow, and what better way to grow than through the stimulation of the arts? That's our gain, our plus: executives who are enriched by this experience and then bring these riches back to their job with them."

The arts, Yunich adds, gain also from such a mutual interdependence, through the contribution that businessmen can so effectively make in the administrative and managerial help the arts so often and so vitally need.

Ralph Burgard, director of state and community relations of the Associated Councils of the Arts, suggests in the Haskins and Sells house organ, *H & S Reports,* issued in November, 1968, that certified public accountants could be of great help to struggling arts organizations unable to afford a large staff. Although his article is written for CPAs (the following extract is expanded slightly from the *H & S Reports* wording), it could apply to executives in many other careers:

Fiscal Planning

The accounting practices of such institutions as symphonies, theatres, and museums are likely to be a pastiche of leftover systems inherited from past administrators or board members with a background in banking. When one considers that the average term of a performing arts administrator is approxi-

99

mately three years, it is easier to understand why uniform accounting procedures are as yet unknown to arts organizations.

Accountants may set up the books, draft a budget form that is intelligible to the board, or establish an efficient system of accounting for contributions to the annual fund campaign.

Rapidly expanding arts institutions are finding it necessary to plan far ahead of the current fiscal year. However, translating five-year artistic goals into budgetary terms is an unfamiliar process to most arts administrators and a skilled accountant could be of the greatest help in this area, even if he is tone deaf.

The community arts councils sponsor cooperative programs involving a number of arts organizations. These projects include developing new audiences for the arts through central promotions, building an arts center, planning a school program in all the arts, or sponsoring an annual united arts fund campaign. The central budget committees for these campaigns function in much the same way as their counterparts in health and welfare. They require people with a thorough fiscal background who can interpret audits and budgets. All budget commitments need at least one accountant volunteering his time in this capacity.

Tax Advice

Arts institutions that qualify as tax exempt must cope with an increasing stream of government report forms, including the annual 990-A return, the state fund campaign registration form, withholding, social security, and entertainment tax exemption forms.

The plight of individual artists is also important here. They have been placed on this earth to enrich our lives by creating music, paintings, sculpture, plays, dances and films. We should not expect them to include among their talents a knowledge of IRS forms.

Rubin Gorewitz, a New York CPA, is well known in the artistic com-

munity as a financial advisor to artists. He recently recalled a time when he had tried to persuade John Cage, the world famous composer, to learn more about fiscal administration for the benefit of an organization on whose board they both served. Cage gently replied that he had 40 years of uncompleted artistic projects in his head and only 20 years left to live. Gorewitz did not try to refute this disarming logic.

There are few creative artists who do not need advice on virtually every aspect of their financial affairs. The accountant can act as the liaison between the artist and his fiscal world. Advice can include preparation of annual returns, establishing a simplified record system for tax purposes or drafting a foundation presentation, a process somewhat analogous to the preparation of an SEC prospectus.

Gorewitz warns that the accountant should not teach the artist accounting. This will only confuse and disturb both artist and accountant. In effect, the accountant assumes the role of fiscal advisor so the artists can devote more time to that which they do best—their art.

Management Counsel

In the administration affairs of organizations and individuals good judgement is an essential ingredient. Accountants, trained in the analytical approach to problem solving, can use this to great advantage in arts administration. They may help the administrator to cope with costing problems or prepare a foundation proposal. They may also exert valuable leadership as members of the boards of directors.

Michael Newton, executive director of The Arts and Education Council of Greater St. Louis, has, according to Burgard, the highest praise for the contributions to St. Louis cultural life of Homer Sayad, a senior partner in Haskins and Sells' St. Louis office. Since he came to St. Louis 14 years ago he has served as president of the St. Louis Opera Theatre and chairman of the Budget Committee of the Arts and Education Council, of which he has been

101

president since 1965. Newton also feels that accountants can render great service to arts organizations because they "think in an orderly fashion and may also act as a bridge between the arts organizations and potential sources of funds."

So could any corporate executive.

3. PARTICIPATION IN PRODUCTIONS

When an executive actually participates in productions of artistic creations he has reached the deepest involvement he can normally achieve. At that stage he becomes, to all intents, an artist himself, at least in that he begins to see how the artists with whom he is working think and feel. There is also the reverse benefit which the executive-artist relationship receives free of charge: the artist begins to see how the businessman thinks.

Participation in the arts need not be more than amateur. Both Dwight Eisenhower and Winston Churchill took up painting as a hobby. Amateur string quartets spend ecstatic evenings at each other's homes arguing over Beethoven's Opus 135. By far the largest number of American orchestras are largely or totally amateur, giving two or five concerts a year. If only 35 of this nation's dramatic theatres are professional, who could possibly make up the nearly 5,000 remainder except amateurs?

4. ORGANIZATION AND ADMINISTRATION OF ARTS INSTITUTION

Joseph Taubman, in the above-mentioned review article for *The Tulane Law Review,* "Performing Arts—The Economic Dilemma," finds some interesting tax possibilities in the corporate establishment of an arts organization:

102

"A business organization might be permitted to have nonprofit cultural divisions or subsidiaries. By analogy to unrelated income taxation of exempt organizations, business enterprise should be able to engage in nonprofit activity provided that no profits inure therefrom to the parent. Such a division should be eligible for tax exemption and contributions thereto to a tax deduction. Business could then make a direct contribution to promote cultural development without fear of running afoul of the limitations of Sections 170 and 162 of the Internal Revenue Laws. Assets and income remaining upon liquidation would not be distributed to the profit-making parent, but to a successor nonprofit division or subsidiary, organization under rules to be promulgated by the Treasury or legislative elaboration of an applicable *cy pres* doctrine under local laws."

Furthermore, according to Taubman, "a business organization might obtain a deduction for subsidizing a performing arts enterprise as ancillary to the trade or business if the charitable deduction of 5% were otherwise exceeded, if the subsidy somehow enhanced the image or goodwill of the organization, on the analogy of institutional advertising."

Whether or not they are taking advantage of the tax possibilities of such a situation, a number of corporations are employing, organizing or managing arts groups to further their recruiting of future executives from college campuses. In a *Wall Street Journal* article in April, 1968, Clayton R. Sutton reported that corporations, in an effort "to win the respect of idealistic youth . . . are trying to show they support cultural and humane values as well as the profit motive." TRW, Inc., of Cleveland, is presenting a one-man stage play, "By George," depicting the life of George Bernard Shaw, free on forty campuses across the country in the 1968-1969 school year. Simon Ramo, TRW vice chairman, calls this "an experimental approach to educational relations." He adds that the company had been looking for "innovative ways of communicating with campus communities" and decided to enlist the performing arts.

103

Other companies using the cultural technique for recruiting include the Mead Corporation, Aluminum Corporation of America, General Electric Company, Motorola, Inc. and Olin Mathieson Chemical Corporation. Alcoa put 60 pieces from its collection of contemporary art on a tour of colleges and company plant cities, keeping its college recruiters informed of the itinerary so they can mention it appropriately as evidence of the company's cultural interests.

C. STIMULATION

This topic is not to deal with stimulation of the arts themselves; rather, its focus is on the stimulation of other than artists to interest in local artistic activities. It can hopefully be assumed that the reader has already been convinced of the necessity of what are loosely called the arts in his community. Remaining is the call to evangelism, the exhortation to others to go and do likewise.

Involvement in persuading support of the arts through example is as old as history. Through the ages the leaders of men have encouraged, supported and, in a large and general sense, directed trends of the arts. Often such encouragement was sheer caprice, as in the eras of papal and grand duke patronage. But some of the works brought forth for these leaders transcend their times and the ages.

In a letter to the Associated Councils of the Arts for publication in *Cultural Affairs,* Richard M. Nixon wrote recently:

> *Art is the most profound and ultimately the most sacred form of freedom of expression that we have. Within its depths and its mysteries is the source of new ways of looking at the world and at ourselves. Nothing we do to foster artistic creativity should tend to directly or indirectly influence artistic content; everything we do to aid the artist and his art should be done to enlarge, not restrict, the area of freedom which is the essence of the artistic experience.*

And Hubert H. Humphrey, in a parallel letter, also published by *Cultural Affairs,* commented:

> *The artist can render a great public service because of his unique talent. I do not believe the artists' politics or attitudes on specific public policies should prevent them from serving. Service should not be construed as evidence that*

105

an artist supports all the policies of the Government, nor should the Government insist on such support from artists any more than it does from other public employees or consultants.

The leaders of present-day America who support and encourage the arts tend to be more conservative than capricious. But their stature and their potential for influence is at least as great as any Grand Duke of the Middle Ages could conceive, much less hope for. Members of the Business Committee for the Arts, listed in the Appendix, represent the largest and most influential corporations in the most powerful nation the world has ever known. They as a body and individually not only support the arts themselves but also encourage others to such support. They believe that "Art is the most profound and ultimately the most sacred form of freedom of expression that we have." They believe that "The artist can render a great public service because of his unique talent." And it is for that reason—and many others as well—that they not only lend their names to the roster of BCA membership but also actively participate in various arts activities in their own localities and across the land.

1. BUSINESS CABINETS

In an increasing number of cities businessmen are forming "business councils," "business committees," and similar groups for dedicated support of the arts. Sam Cooper, president of HumKo Products in Memphis, wrote of one such experience in the inaugural issue, April, 1968, *BCA News*, telling how they did it and stimulating similar interest among other businessmen in other cities in his article, "Reviving the Arts—The Memphis Story!"

"About five years ago the Memphis Arts Council was formed. It had a difficult time getting established successfully and received very little recognition and support, especially from business. Two years ago it was at its lowest ebb and floundering.

"At that time a small group of businessmen, realizing the importance of strengthening our cultural organizations, banded together in an effort to generate interest and support from the business community. An idea was conceived to form a Cabinet of fifty business leaders and, surprisingly, to a man, from the first fifty calls a Cabinet was born.

"These men were asked at the front end to provide financial support and also to participate in the campaign fund. Furthermore, they were expected to take an interest and, when called upon, to become active in the operation of the Council and its member organizations. A number of them were elected to the Board of the Council and others became involved with various artistic groups. By their involvement things began to happen. First of all, the Council was told by the Cabinet that if it expected its support, each organization had to conduct its affairs in a business-like manner, which several were not doing. Members of the Cabinet provided guidance and leadership in bringing this about.

"The Council itself began to function as though it were a private enterprise in handling its planning, budgets and finances. The development of the Cabinet had good publicity, which served several purposes. It made the Cabinet Member realize his importance in the project and at the same time the entire program was exposed to the community at large. Once it was apparent that the business leaders were going to give full support to the arts, the public was encouraged to do its part by patronage.

"Prior to the formation of the Cabinet two years ago the Council's drive raised about 80% of its $100,000 goal. The following year a goal with the Cabinet functioning was established at $125,000 and actually $145,000 was raised. As soon as the goal went over the top the drive lost momentum and many businesses were not approached. Had they been, there is no question but what we would have been able to obtain more money. This past year the Cabinet was confronted with a challenge of a $400,000 matching fund from the Ford Foundation for the Memphis

107

Orchestral Society as well as the need of a $200,000 general fund drive and succeeded in raising the $600,000.

"From our experience, we think the following major points are worthy of consideration by a business committee formed to support the arts.

"1. Each community form a Cabinet (or similar organization) of business leaders to give direction and support the arts.

"2. Each major city (or area) have an Arts Council with one over-all drive for its member organizations.

"3. Emphasis be placed on employing directors who are capable of executive leadership and maintaining interest in the Cabinet for fund-raising purposes as well as coordinating activities of the Arts Council.

"4. Each state form a state-wide Business Cabinet . . . (in addition to liaison with the National Business Committee for the Arts, it can also be influential with the State Legislatures for financial support of the arts at a local level)."

2. FUND-RAISING

Other businessmen band together in raising funds for the arts, perhaps in one of the united arts fund drives in the 18 (soon to be more) cities that have already established them, perhaps in some other and more experimental drive. Alvin H. Reiss wrote of some of the current activities of this nature in the Summer, 1968 issue of *Arts Management* that cultural groups are opening donors' pocketbooks and winning attention in their communities by adding a few frills and twists to the old-fashioned American auction. One such is held in Boston for the benefit of educational television station KGBH. The third annual event raised $282,000, more than five per cent of the station's yearly operating budget. The auction was presented on the air for 7 consecutive evenings, with viewers phoning in their bids

Stanford Calderwood, Vice-President Polaroid Corporation, is auctioneer for educational television station WGBH-TV fund-raising drive.

Norman Rabb, Director Stop & Shop Corporation, also acted as auctioneer in the successful drive.

for the merchandise they saw televised. The participation of the Boston area's top businessmen assured the event's success. Not only did corporations donate nearly all the merchandise—6,000 items ranging up to $25,000 in retail price were offered in the most recent auction—but their board chairmen, presidents and vice presidents acted as on-the-air auctioneers.

A committee of prominent St. Louis civic, business and cultural leaders was recently involved in finding unusual gifts for its local auction, "Cultural Auction of Many Extraordinary Lots of Treasure," or CAMELOT. The event, under the general sponsorship of the Famous-Barr department store, benefits The Arts and Education Council of Greater St. Louis and its associated cultural activities. Among the items auctioned were a chance to conduct the St. Louis Symphony Orchestra for an evening, a guided tour of Cape Kennedy, a party's background guitar music by James Symington, former Chief of Protocol of the State Department, and a Chinese dinner cooked by Danny Kaye. The sum raised by this means was $175,000.

According to Reiss, similar auctions in San Diego, Seattle (PONCHO) and Portland, Oregon have raised more than $100,000 each for cultural groups. Seattle's PONCHO auction was, in fact, so successful that its organizer, Paul S. Friedlander, president of Friedlander and Sons, was invited to St. Louis to help them with their CAMELOT.

The various methods and examples of supporting the arts discussed above in this Part III can only give some idea of the possibilities that have already been considered and acted upon. Any corporate executive can think of many other ideas that have not been mentioned, examples that have not been given. Whatever the means used in helping and identifying with the arts, it is the result that finally counts: the recognition of the arts and business as integral parts of the same society. There could be no better way to emphasize the importance of encouragement and stimulation of the arts than to quote the words of John F. Kennedy on the subject:

Art and the encouragement of art is political in the most profound sense, not as a weapon in a struggle, but as an instrument of understanding of the futility of struggle between those who share men's faith. Aeschylus and Plato are remembered today long after the triumphs of imperial Athens are gone. Dante outlived the ambitions of 13th century Florence. Goethe stands serenely above the politics of Germany, and I am certain that after the dust of centuries has passed over our cities, we, too, will be remembered not for our victories or defeats in battle or politics, but for our contribution to the human spirit.

111

PART FOUR:
THE OUTLOOK

While cautious optimism is the most sanguine attitude that has been expressed by most knowledgeable observers in appraisal of the future of the business and the arts relationship and some, like Princeton professors Baumol and Bowen in their study for the Twentieth Century Fund, have been frankly pessimistic, still it is hard to see how this movement can go any way but up.

The trend toward increased leisure time is inexorable. The war on poverty, while slowed by the misadventure in Vietnam, will surely be renewed; the percentage of the population obtaining higher education, up steadily since 1900 and sensationally since World War II, will continue to rise; the electronic media will be driven to supply more substantial fare as the price of holding the attention of an increasingly sophisticated public; the increasing availability of copying facilities and devices, which have already made this the Age of Facsimile, will make art an even bigger business than it has already become; the trend toward mixed media will make more kinds of art available in more kinds of places; the increased importance of design, already heightened by greater consumer sophistication, will continue to bring art and business into close relationship. These are only a few of the many indices that the arts will become increasingly important to an increasing percentage of a growing population. Art will become more and more relevant to business, and vice versa. Already there are cases where it's hard to see the old lines of demarcation.

How would you classify the success of an Andy Warhol? Is it business or is it art? For that matter, whether or not you consider Picasso the greatest artist of our time, as many do, it would be hard to think of another figure in the art world even remotely comparable to him as a businessman.

But scoffing and miffing at any aspect of art today, at a time when the arts are in ferment as never before, is as pointless and futile as it was to jeer and make jokes about the steamboat, the locomotive and the automobile. Art will continue to crop out in new forms, just as energy has, and every time it does, the relevance of all art to the lives of all of us is by just that much increased.

It is easy to make fun of such expressions as "the culture boom" on the ground that it is a contradiction in terms. And it is always tempting, when looking over the entire cultural complex of our day, and attempting to measure the stature of our poets and playwrights and composers and writers and painters and sculptors against that of the greatest of the past, to leap to the conclusion that, in such matters at least, things were better when they were worse.

It is easy to ascribe to inflation a large part of the enormous increase in spending for the arts that has occurred over the past ten or fifteen years and to dismiss as "amateur" a large part of the expansion in number and kinds of arts groups over the same period.

A lesson that many businesses have come to learn, and sometimes the hard way, is never to underestimate the importance of the amateur, the enthusiast, the hobbyist. Detroit, for instance, dismissed as the lunatic fringe of the car market those car buffs who kept harping on features they found only in imported cars, until the foreign cars made such serious inroads into the domestic market that Detroit was at last constrained to listen. As a result, the sporty cars named after wild beasts, fish, and horses, soon were selling in the hundreds of thousands, at least tenfold beyond the sales in this country of their imported prototypes. Small beginnings have a way of mushrooming, when enough dedicated amateurs begin talking up their enthusiasms.

Considered also must be the possibility that large numbers of our present hordes of Sunday painters, spare time fiddlers and amateur actors may be businessmen, and allowance must be made for the possibility that each of them becomes an emissary of enthusiasm, for at least one of the arts, into the ranks of business.

By the same token, allowance should also be made for the infectiousness of the enthusiasm of businessmen upon the promotional tactics and techniques of the arts groups into which they infiltrate. We have seen the lift given to the opera in Seattle, through the application of what to many people must have seemed shockingly "hard sell." Who's to say how often this may happen elsewhere, whether in opera, symphony, theatre or dance, where some enthusiast gets on the board who happens to be a demon promoter or public relations genius, and starts to hypo the box-office with appeals much broader than the previous time-honored practice of preaching only to the converted?

Imagine the consternation among the old guard under whose austere patronage, and thanks to whose benign checks, the symphony led its sheltered life in the past, if some zany promoter were to start putting out bumper stickers proclaiming in Day-Glo letters that "Symphony Swings" and buttons or even sweatshirts bearing the impudent tidings that "Beethoven is Boss." Unimaginable in the past, such tactics may be old-hat in the fairly near future.

The point is simply that the arts today can and do look much farther afield, both for audience and for support, than the narrow confines of the Horseshoe Circle, the day of whose dominance is as dated as that of the horse itself as the prime means of transport.

Let me hark back to Ralph Burgard's dictum, in *Arts in the City,* about people in ghetto areas needing music but not symphony concerts. This in its context was a sensible statement. It took realistic consideration of the forces that are pressing upon the arts, both from within and from without, to break down their old rigid and formal compartmentalization. It also understood that in our present permissive and topsy-turvy society the arts are not going to stay put, whether we

117

like it or not. Whatever boxes we provide for them, whether in the form of auditoriums, museums, libraries, culture centers or what not, the arts will be mobile.

On the other hand, Henry Lewis, the Negro conductor of the New Jersey Symphony, is equally sensible, on precisely the opposite side of Burgard's cited example of the symphony and the ghetto. Writing in *The New York Times* on July 7, 1968 of his plans to give a series of concerts "right smack in the middle of the Newark ghetto, on an empty lot in fact," he said: "There are some Negroes in the ghetto who say, 'What do we need with a symphony concert? That's white man's music.' When I first heard this attitude I was quite shocked. I just couldn't imagine that anyone could reject symphonic music 'because it has nothing to do with us.' I don't believe that a Negro can't enjoy, for example, Schubert's 'Unfinished' Symphony because it's 'white man's music.' It's music about feelings and hurt and sorrow and tragedy and love and happiness, and these things transcend racial or ethnic barriers . . . Eventually, the goal of these concerts in an empty lot is to dissipate the feeling that most Negroes who live in the ghetto have that they do not belong in Newark's Symphony Hall."

To the symphonic musician, accustomed as any waiter to the occupational necessity of wearing evening dress clothes every night, playing in an empty lot may seem strange. Mark Twain once expressed envy of the symphonic man, saying in effect that his was a job like any other, but what a job! What may lie ahead for symphony players, in this new era of mixed media, is presaged in another column, by Donal Henahan, in the same issue of *The New York Times:* "In increasing numbers and with increasing success, modern composers are discovering how to make the artistic quantum leap of our time: from the academic avant-garde to what may be called, for want of a more precise term, the avant-groove. That is they are abandoning the relatively recent European tradition of the artist as anti-popular prophet for the more ancient conception of the artist as a man deeply involved in contemporary society.

"The situation that has prodded such academically trained composers out of the traditional way of looking at music and its uses was brought into sharp focus not long ago, when George Crumb won the 1967 Pulitzer Prize in music for his multi-media work, *Echoes of Time and the River*. Commissioned by the University of Chicago, the Crumb piece has been played exactly twice (under great protest from some orchestra men) by the Chicago Symphony.

"Crumb, who teaches composition at the University of Pennsylvania, requires of orchestra members that they not only play their instruments in outlandish ways (a percussionist lowers a gong into a bucket of water, for instance, to bend the pitch slightly), but to chant meaningless phrases in unison, to whistle in chords, and to march about in ritualistic processionals. All this, of course, veers far off the symphonic music path, and merges with pure theatre. Few orchestras will be willing to put such fare before their old subscribers when a Brahms-Beethoven program can be rehearsed and presented with one-tenth the effort and cost, and ten times the chance of acceptance. In fact, Crumb's only real audience, like that of so many other restless academics these days, waits outside halls where music is treated like a Ming vase, to be put under a glass bell and admired once or twice a week in reverential surroundings."

That such things could emanate from such places as the University of Chicago and the University of Pennsylvania will strike the hard-shell businessman, educated only in the College of Hard Knocks, as proof positive that at last the inmates have taken over the asylum. But such businessmen are being phased out faster, even, than these new trends are crashing in from all sides of the art world today. The new breed of young businessmen is much more likely than yesterday's breed of old artists to think that such things are wonderful.

With the arts changing as much as everything else around us is changing these days, it would take only the very brave or the very stupid to attempt to assay, with any certainty, what will or won't take place in our concert halls and on

119

our stages and screens, and in our galleries and museums, and in the pages of our books and magazines, on a very near tomorrow.

The phrase "restless academics" in Henahan's column is the operative expression. Only yesterday such a combination of words would have constituted a contradiction in terms. The "academic" was the settled and quiet and contemplative and pastoral, and the "groves of academe" was practically synonymous with cloistered and sequestered, in the pursuit of pure learning in a spirit that was indeed the very antonym of "restless." But in that fairly recent day students, like artists, were not expected to be "deeply involved in contemporary society." For that matter, neither were businessmen, as recently as the heyday of Babbitt, which coincided with the quiet time of Cal Coolidge.

The status of the business and the arts movement today is in the stage of simple arithmetic, whereas tomorrow and sooner or later thereafter it may achieve the successive levels of geometry, trigonometry and calculus. Today it is simple enough and in a sufficiently early stage to be fairly well summed up in a new set of Three R's.

The first of these Three R's is Relevance. Art has become much more relevant to our daily lives than was ever true in the past. Not only is art in all its forms and many new guises much more readily and widely available to all of us, through new media of communication as well as through the new tendencies to mix media and to take the art to the public in many instances, among which are cited the Jazzmobile and the concerts in the parks. Also there is more and better art in our lives today through the greatly increased importance of the role of the designer, in all forms of merchandising and even at the lowest price levels. Both advertising and merchandising forces have long since come to realize the effectiveness of beauty as a business tool, with the result that over the years, and particularly of late, business and the arts have been brought closer together.

120

The second of these Three R's is Recruitment. Business has lost ground with the youth of today. The young men of talent and promise can no longer be taken for granted as logical prospects for recruitment into the ranks of business. It's a common phenomenon today for the businessman to find that his son not only looks on his business, but also on the town where that business is conducted, with disdain. He'd so much rather do something interesting, in and of itself, in some place far enough away to enjoy the glamour that only distance confers—better the Peace Corps in some newly emergent country you never heard of than to stick to business in Chicago or Pittsburgh or Keokuk or Where Have You.

One answer to this reluctance of youth to look on both business and the old hometown with any but a jaded eye is to try to invest both with some of the glamour that rubs off from involvement with the arts. One of the most revealing and significant sections of the Rockefeller Panel Report, *The Performing Arts: Problems and Prospects*, cites instances where there was a direct ratio between the ease or the difficulty in recruiting talent for business enterprises, depending on the presence or the absence of cultural attractions in the community. (Some of the twenty-three states that up to now have given their arts councils little or no money ought to think about that.)

The third of the new Three R's is perhaps less immediately self-evident. It is Respect. There's a new respect for the arts, as well as a new respect for education in many businesses today. The former attitude was that anything learned in college or enjoyed for its own sake, that had no immediate bearing on the job in hand, was something that had to be put out of mind as fast as possible. In the old days, when the self-made man was a far more familiar figure in management than he is today, this was almost universal. But the ranks of management are increasingly filled by men who either have been educated to an interest in the arts and a respect for them, or have acquired it as collectors or even as practitioners. Most of the

121

latter are amateurs, though those of near-professional competence are by no means as rare as might be supposed.

In any case, much of the genuine interest in and respect for the arts that has come to permeate management levels as a logical concomitant of "the culture boom," may be taken simply to stand for the new emphasis on arts and creativity which has characterized the sixties in contrast to the emphasis on science and research that was the counterpart in the fifties. It is this which has tended to give the arts and all appeals connected with arts projects a new respectability in the executive suites. Even those occupants who still have neither interest nor appreciation now would pause before admitting the lack, although once they would have bellowed it out without hesitation or any twinge of self-consciousness.

So call it Respect, or call it Respectability. It amounts to the same thing, because there's a certain and growing bandwagon aspect to the current involvement of business with the arts.

The term "bandwagon" is used, of course, purely in a relative sense, for while the time is long gone when the involvement of a businessman in the arts was considered a presence as incongruous as that of a cop in a ballet, still the men of affairs who sense the significance of the arts in the long-run improvement of the quality of life in their communities constitute a minority. It is a hearteningly increasing minority, but it would be less than honest to suggest that such awareness on the part of business is now the rule rather than the exception, increasingly frequent though that exception may be, and in fact is, compared to only a brief three or four years back.

While it would be fatuous to propound that artists and businessmen, as a whole and as a class, have overnight fallen into an ecstatic state of brotherly love, still it would be equally wide of the truth to state that, categorically, they still look at each other like strange bulldogs.

Probably it would be fair to say that everybody mentioned in these pages deserves, to greater or lesser degree, to be considered something of a pioneer. The movement is barely out of its Indian-fighting days, but the moment of the establishment of the Business Committee for the Arts, as a business-based counterpart to the arts-based Associated Council of the Arts, could well be likened to the day when the last spike was driven in the tracks to link the two coasts and signify the closing of the last frontier.

On the immediate and short-term basis, the forecast for the weather ahead could well be "partly cloudy to cloudy, with bright intervals," even though the long-range outlook is beyond a doubt very good.

Contributing to the cloudy aspect of the short-term outlook is the fact that the prospect of substantial government aid, hailed with such fanfare just a few years back, has gone into momentary eclipse. The Yahoo congressman may well be a vanishing breed, but the day of his extinction is not yet arrived.

Also a factor is the crisis aspect of the urban problem, with the unrest in the cities conferring a higher priority on the emissary of an organization concerned with better jobs and training programs for non-whites than any that can be realistically expected currently to be accorded someone attempting to raise money for the arts. The one exception on that front, of course, is the time-honored tactic of "If you can't lick 'em, join 'em," in the form of working up arts programs purely on their value and virtue as ghetto-condition palliatives and ameliorants. This is bad even when it's good, as the arts should be able to stand up on their own and be counted as among the positive attributes to overall community enrichment, and not snuck in disguised as tranquilizers of turbulence.

In the long run, the role that the arts must play is one of helping to make life more tolerable for us all, by relief of some of the stresses and strains that make modern living equally hard on the nerves and tempers of rich and poor.

123

Because of the one thing the Supreme Court said in 1954 having to do with "all deliberate speed," something else it said the same year has had less attention than it might otherwise have received. In Parker v. Berman, October, 1954, the Supreme Court said:

"The concept of the public welfare is broad and inclusive. The values it represents are spiritual as well as physical, aesthetic as well as monetary. It is within the power of the legislature to determine that the community should be beautiful as well as healthy, spacious as well as clean, well-balanced as well as carefully patrolled."

In the enlightened purview of business, in its relations to the community in which it operates, all of these considerations will ultimately have a place. It is only recently that business has begun to show a more than occasional and exceptional awareness of this widened concept of the public welfare. As one of its first manifestations, after business' general recognition of the importance of education, has come this dawning realization of the importance of the arts. There can be no question that ultimately this awareness will be as general as it is today remarkable. The point already reached, as indicated by the variety and number of the instances cited to date, can certainly be considered well over that imaginary line of demarcation that marks "the end of the beginning."

As there is increasing recognition of this widened concept of the public welfare, business will give the arts their due share of its support and involvement. Nor will it stop with the arts. In the relentless onward march of mechanization and automation, business will ultimately arrive at an almost frightened concern for the individual. This will be dramatized by events, probably not too distant, that will serve to underline the increasingly serious plight of us all, as concerns water and air pollution, and the desperate necessity for noise-abatement. The New York area has already experienced killer-fogs of Londonlike severity. There can conceivably be a "breath-out" that will be as dramatic as the blackout was in November of '65. Such events will dramatize the importance of these other concerns, as suddenly and effectively as the first flash of Sputnik over our skies in the fall of 1957 gave an emergency emphasis to the importance of education.

This concern for the individual will extend to the inner as well as the outer man. In short, everything that concerns the individual will be recognized as the concern of business. To support the library, for instance, will be seen to be at least as important as to support "the college of your choice." That the money will be forthcoming to support the arts can almost be taken for granted, because the momentum is now well established. But it will have to be followed by money for a lot of other things, too, that up to now have not figured importantly among the concerns of business. For how can the arts flourish, however well supported, in an environment where the air and the water are made foul with waste?

Art, like nature, abhors a vacuum, which is what some of our central cities will soon become if present tendencies and trends are permitted to continue unabated. And as for business—well, in a vacuum, where it can't exist, business simply vanishes. So business will soon see its responsibility for supporting a lot of projects for the curing of environmental ailments that it never had to think about before. Indiscriminate urban sprawl, spoliation of natural resources, and heedless interference with the ecology—these are things that have been going on for so long, and with so little notice of them, that businessmen as a whole and as a class are going to wake up to their ominous significance with a start. And here, again, support for the arts, however well established as a principle and a practice, may go into sudden and at least partial eclipse, overshadowed by more panicky priorities.

In the long run, the money will be found for all these concerns, first because it will have to be, and second because it's there. But each time a new cause takes on a suddenly urgent priority, as right now with urban disorders, there will undoubtedly be another cloudy period for the support of the arts. When there are fires to be put out, so to speak, there's always the consolation that "culture can wait."

That the money is there, there are all sorts of figures to indicate. The last full-year figures that the Rockefeller Panel Report on the performing arts could reflect were those for 1963. In the next three years, corporate philanthropic allocations of all kinds went up by nearly forty per cent, from the $536 million total in 1963 to $750 million in 1966. But the ratio of contributions to corporate net income remained constant, hovering around one per cent, although the government allows deductions of up to five per cent for philanthropy. But according to a NICB survey, the share of civic and cultural contributions went up, by nearly sixty per cent, from 5.3 per cent in 1962 to 8.3 per cent in 1965. There's the basis for such guarded optimism as has been expressed. This was the highest percentage of all corporate philanthropy that these two areas, civic and cultural, had ever registered, and it caused the National Industrial Conference Board to list them separately, for the first time. This showed that cultural activities claimed 2.8 per cent of total corporate giving in 1965, or roughly twenty-two and a half million dollars. Despite such large gifts as the half million given to the Metropolitan Opera by Eastern Airlines for the new production of the Wagnerian Ring cycle, and the three hundred thousand given by Bristol-Myers for a series of programs on the arts to Channel 13, the educational television station in New York, the best guesstimates still do not rise appreciably above twenty-five million as the current total for corporate giving to the arts.

But the really big increase in this total that can be expected to materialize from here on out will undoubtedly come as indirect consequences, rather than as directly causative factors, of the growing business involvement with the arts. Unless and until businessmen in appreciable numbers had begun to evince considerable interest in the arts, little of the present impressive evidence of corporate support would ever have been forthcoming. The major increases will occur, as naturally as day follows night, only as more and more businessmen become more and more interested.

And this is what's happening.

That's why we may have been mistaken in giving such emphasis to our own "$250,000,000 Equation" in publicizing *Esquire's* Business in the Arts awards. Much more realistic was the attitude of the Business Committee for the Arts, as expressed by its chairman, Douglas Dillon, of not pressuring anybody for anything, and simply letting the force of example exert itself. We were trying, of course, to dramatize what an enormous increase could be brought about in corporate support of the arts, well within the current confines of tax deductibility, if only business were to earmark for the arts just half of one per cent of its net income instead of the approximately one twenty-fifth of one per cent that was the prevailing figure at the time of the Rockefeller Report's revelation that business was giving to the arts less than "a nickel on the dollar" of all its philanthropy.

According to the same statisticians who worked up the original figures for the Rockefeller Panel Report on the performing arts, if corporations could have been persuaded to take even half the five per cent deduction permitted by the federal governmnt in applying the corporate income tax, an additional one billion two hundred million dollars would have moved into the coffers of America's charitable and educational institutions in 1966 alone. So the total of two hundred fifty million yearly for the arts from business, that we projected in 1966 as a goal, is not as fantastic as it sounded to some at the time. Actually, the arts now receive at least that much from all fund sources, but a bare tenth of it now comes from business. Individual giving to the arts has in recent years run well over two hundred million dollars, or better than a dollar per capita, whereas federal giving,

127

for the first three years of the activities of the National Endowment for the Arts, worked out to a mere 3.5 cents per capita. Even that much direct federal aid to the arts has been decreasing annually. Of course, if such pessimistic estimates are to be believed as were made by Baumol and Bowen in their report for the Twentieth Century Fund (that only four per cent of the population are ever exposed to any live performances of the performing arts), then the 3.5 cents per capita figure would be just about right. But with all the outdoor concerts that are now given all summer long all over the land, it is hard to believe that the symphonies alone are not heard by more than the eight million that the four per cent figure now comprises. If four hundred of our more than fourteen hundred orchestras are heard by no more than twenty thousand people each, in the course of a year, there's the eight million, and certainly the audiences in Central Park and at Hollywood Bowl run many times twenty thousand in the course of a summer, to say nothing of new places like the Blossom Center between Cleveland and Akron.

If both business and government support could be brought up to parity with the present level of individual giving then the arts would be on easy street. The chances that this level will be achieved within the measurably near future by business are much better than they are for anything like comparable government support. President Johnson for once left no credibility gap whatever when he said, upon signing the Arts and Humanities Bill in 1965:

"We in America have not always been kind to the artists and the scholars who are the creators and the keepers of our vision. Somehow, the scientists always seem to get the penthouse, while the arts and the humanities get the basement."

That this will change very much seems unlikely, short of that fair day when the meek shall at last inherit the earth. But at least in this decade, since the end of the Eisenhower administration, the arts have had a much greater share of the national attention than has been true since the time of Thomas Jefferson. In large part this is ascribable to the fact that in the last decade the arts have become big business, to a degree that was never even envisioned in the past. It is enough to glance through a recent book, *Buying Art on a Budget,* by Joanna Reese, to realize how suddenly and to what an extent art has dug in across America. Where only yesterday it was the preserve of a handful of galleries seeking to interest a few fat cats in the acquisition of old masters, today it is a grass-roots affair, with install-ment buying and rentals with options to purchase, and an infinity of schools and types of art and artifacts to collect. The chances of an ordinary businessman's being bitten by the art bug and becoming a gallery goer and an auction shopper are much greater than ever before. People seem to go to galleries now as commonly and as casually as they used to go to the movies. Suddenly art is everywhere, and it seems that everything is art, from junk sculpture to found objects, and that nothing is too obscure or out of the way to attract a devoted band of enthusiastic collectors.

It is this, more than anything else, that will ultimately bring about a much more intimate involvement of business with the arts than anything we have seen to date, as one by one more and more businessmen become addicted to the arts. A man's hobby colors his whole life, and it seeks means of gratification, or sub-limation or transference, beyond the arbitrary limits of his leisure hours. He will find ways and means to express it, sometimes even subconsciously, in the course of the pursuit of his workaday tasks. Given an aroused interest in any one of the arts, an arts coloration will subsequently show up in more and more of his business activities, whether in such likely places as advertising and public relations or in such unlikely places as incentive plans, sales contests, or office parties and outings.

More often than not, a man's interest in an art form is fortuitous, his first exposure incurred through more or less reluctant attendance at an event that his

129

wife wouldn't miss but about which he himself thought he couldn't care less. The wife is often sorry afterward, when he with the convert's usual superheated zeal becomes a fanatic on the subject in which she had never herself had more than a casual and largely social interest. If it's one where there is an element of collecting involved, the family record will suddenly change, and where the amounts previously invested were never more than pin money, they will multiply to major proportions.

Whenever this happens his business will inevitably reflect, in some more or less direct way, his own newfound enthusiasm. If he's an executive, no matter how junior, he will sooner or later influence company policy to favor his choice among the arts. And if he's the big boss, and the chances are more than even that he might be, and he's suddenly discoverd, say, ballet, in next to no time at all he'll have a good portion of the company going around in pirouettes and balancing on their toes.

When this happens often enough, and it's happening every day all over America, then nobody will have to sit up nights watching to see if the figures go up on corporate support of the arts. Increased support will be a natural consequence of increased involvement.

The fact that there are so many more art forms now than there were before only increases the likelihood of the more rapid spread of this kind of infection. Who's to say today, with any certainty, just what is and isn't art? Just as practically anything is a business, so virtually everything is an art. This new fluidity was well expressed in the 1968 Art Directors' Club conference in New York, where Henry Wolf devised the theme by drawing two lines, one horizontal and the other vertical, and bounding them with four words. Time and Money were polarized by the horizontal line, and Art and Love by the vertical. Move the lines either up and down or back and forth, and any way you look at it, you've encompassed everything we do and seek and value and strive for. Use equation marks or ampersands, as you like, or the symbols of multiplication or division. On the playing field of these four forces we all spend our lives. What else is there?

"Art is everything, and everything is art," said the Reverend Ernest Dunkley at a 1968 business and the arts luncheon in New York. He was seeking to explain, to the representatives of the various business-based and arts-based organizations in attendance, the viewpoint of his parishioners in Bedford Stuyvesant, a ghetto area of Brooklyn. To most of those present, he was an emissary from a strange world, a cauldron of vice and violence oddly blended with love and compassion and aspirations common to mankind.

A frequent Bedford-Stuyvesant greeting is "How is everything?" The customary answer is "Everything is everything." It may sound like something out of Lewis Carroll, but in that setting it has a certain dignity and a rather sweet sort of sense. And from that premise his conclusion was beautifully logical.

It has no answer, and it forecloses argument. Art is everything, and everything is art. You can't top that; you can only change the subject. As a statement, it is of a piece with what Ralph Burgard, who was there, calls the "deceptively simple" Balinese one: "We have no art; we do everything as well as we can."

Who among us, artists and businessmen alike, can say more?

ABOUT THE AUTHOR

Arnold Gingrich is as actively involved in the world of the arts as any business-man in America. A University of Michigan Phi Beta Kappa graduate, he is the publisher and founding editor of *Esquire* magazine, Chairman of the Arts Advisory Council, New York Board of Trade; chairman of the board of trustees, New York Orchestral Society; and director of both the American Symphony Orchestra League and the Business Committee for the Arts.

It is no coincidence that with such a background he recently challenged the American business community at a Board of Trade luncheon with a keynote address entitled "Is Culture the Business of Business?" The nationally-known "Business in the Arts" awards, co-sponsored by *Esquire* magazine and the Business Committee for the Arts are further testimony to Mr. Gingrich's dedicated conviction that the two are inseparable necessities if our communities are to thrive.

SELECTED BIBLIOGRAPHY

Andrews, F. Emerson. *Philanthropic Giving*. Russell Sage Foundation, New York, 1950.

Andrews, F. Emerson. *Corporation Giving*. Russell Sage Foundation, New York, 1952.

The Arts: A Central Element of a Good Society. Associated Councils of the Arts, New York, 1965. Various speeches, especially "Corporate Giving" by Fred Lazarus III.

The Arts: Planning for Change. Associated Councils of the Arts, New York, 1966. Various speeches, especially "Industry's Stake in the Arts" by Lucien Wilson.

Baumol, William J. and William G. Bowen. *Performing Arts—The Economic Dilemma*, "A Study of Problems common to Theatre, Opera, Music and Dance." The Twentieth Century Fund, New York, 1966.

Berg, Ivar, ed. *The Business of America*. Harcourt, Brace & World, New York, 1968. Various chapters, especially those in Part 5: "Businessmen and American Culture."

Burgard, Ralph. *Arts in the City*, "Organizing and Programming Community Arts Councils." Associated Councils of the Arts, New York, 1968.

The Conference Board Record, January 1968. National Industrial Conference Board, New York. Especially section on "Philanthropy and the Corporation," with articles by John H. Watson, III, Alfred C. Neal, Manning M. Pattilo, W. Homer Turner and Richard Eells.

Eells, Richard. *The Corporation and the Arts*. Macmillan, New York, 1967.

Eells, Richard. *Corporation Giving in a Free Society*. Harper & Row, New York, 1956.

Eells, Richard. *The Meaning of Modern Business: An Introduction to the Philosophy of Large Corporate Enterprise*. Columbia University Press, New York, 1960. Especially Chapter 4: "The Dilemma of Corporate Responsibility."

The Future of Capitalism. Symposium commemorating the fiftieth anniversary of the National Industrial Conference Board. Macmillan, New York, 1967. Especially "Capitalism, Culture and the Arts" by David Rockefeller.

Golden, L.L.L. *Only by Public Consent*, "American Corporations Search for Favorable Opinion." Hawthorn Books, New York, 1968.

Kahn, Herman and Anthony J. Wiener. *The Year 2000*, "A framework for Speculation on the Next Thirty-three Years." The Hudson Institute. Macmillan, New York, 1967.

Morison, Bradley and Kay Fliehr. *In Search of an Audience*, "How An Audience Was Found for the Tyrone Guthrie Theatre." Pitman, New York, 1968.

133

The Performing Arts: Problems and Prospects, "Rockefeller Panel Report on the future of theatre, dance, music in America." Special Studies Project of the Rockefeller Brothers Fund. McGraw-Hill, New York, 1965.

Readings in Company Contributions. National Industrial Conference Board, New York, 1967.

Russell-Cobb, Trevor. *Paying the Piper,* "The Theory and Practice of Industrial Patronage." Queen Anne Press, London, 1968.

Thomas, Ralph Lingo. *Policies Underlying Corporate Giving.* Prentice-Hall, Englewood Cliffs, New Jersey, 1966.

Toffler, Alvin C. *The Culture Consumers,* "Art and Affluence in America." Penguin, Baltimore, 1965.

Walton, Clarence C. *Corporate Social Responsibilities.* Wadsworth, Belmont, California, 1967.

Walton, Clarence and Richard Eells, eds. *The Business System,* "Readings in Ideas and Concepts." 3 vols. Macmillan, New York, 1965. Various chapters, especially those in Part VI: "Business and the Realm of Values."

BUSINESS COMMITTEE FOR THE ARTS

Akerson, George E. Chairman
        Boston Herald-Traveler Corporation, Boston
Ames, Amyas Chairman, Executive Committee
        Kidder, Peabody Company, Inc., New York
*Ammidon, Hoyt Chairman
        United States Trust Company of New York
Anderson, Robert O. Chairman
        Atlantic Richfield Company, Philadelphia
*Annenberg, Walter President
        Triangle Publications, Inc., Philadelphia
Beinecke, William S. Chairman and President
        The Sperry and Hutchinson Company, New York
Berner, T. Roland Chairman and President
        Curtiss-Wright Corporation, Wood Ridge, New Jersey
Bingham, Barry President and Publisher
        Courier-Journal and Louisville Times Company, Louisville
*Blough, Roger M. Chairman
        United States Steel Corporation, New York
Bronfman, Edgar M. President
        Joseph E. Seagram and Sons, Inc., New York
Burnham, Donald C. President
        Westinghouse Electric Corporation, Pittsburgh
Cabot, Louis W. President
        Cabot Corporation, Boston
Cooper, Sam President
        HumKo Products, Memphis
Cowles, John, Jr. Vice President
        Minneapolis Star and Tribune Company, Minneapolis
Cummings, Nathan Chairman
        Consolidated Foods Corporation, Chicago
Dayton, Kenneth N. Executive Vice President
        Dayton Corporation, Minneapolis
Dillingham, Lowell S. President
        Dillingham Corporation, Honolulu
*Dillon, C. Douglas President
        U.S. and Foreign Securities Corporation, New Jersey

Ingersoll, Robert S. Chairman
Borg-Warner Corporation, Chicago
*Irwin, George M. Chairman
Quincy Compressor Division, Colt Industries, Quincy, Ill.
Jenkins, William M. Chairman
Seattle-First National Bank, Seattle
Johnson, Samuel C. Chairman and President
S. C. Johnson and Son, Inc., Racine, Wisconsin
Jones, John T., Jr. President
Houston Consolidated Television Company, Houston
*Josephs, Devereux C. Director
New York Life Insurance Company, New York
*Kaiser, Edgar F. Chairman
Kaiser Industries Corporation, Oakland
Kennedy, David M. Chairman
Continental Illinois National Bank and Trust Company of Chicago
Loeb, John L. Partner
Loeb, Rhoades and Company, New York
*MacBain, Gavin K. Chairman
Bristol-Myers Company, New York
Marcus, Stanley President
Neiman-Marcus Company, Dallas
Maremont, Arnold H. President
Maremont Corporation, Chicago
May, Morton D. Chairman
The May Department Stores Company, St. Louis
May, William F. Chairman
American Can Company, New York
McCurdy, R. C. President
Shell Oil Company, New York
McElroy, Neil H. Chairman
Procter and Gamble Company, Cincinnati
Mellon, Paul President
National Gallery of Art, Washington, D.C.
Merriam, John F. Chairman Executive Committee
Northern Natural Gas Company, Omaha
Metcalf, Gordon M. Chairman
Sears, Roebuck and Company, Chicago
Meyer, Andre Senior Partner
Lazard Freres and Company, New York
Miller, Arjay R. Vice Chairman
Ford Motor Company, Dearborn

137

*Miller, J. Irwin Chairman
    Cummins Engine Company, Inc., Columbus, Indiana
Miller, Otto N. Chairman
    Standard Oil Company of California, San Francisco
Moore, George S. Chairman
    First National City Bank, New York
Murphy, Franklin D. Chairman
    Times Mirror Company, Los Angeles
Myers, Charles F., Jr. President
    Burlington Industries, Inc., Greensboro, N.C.
Nickerson, Albert L. Chairman
    Mobil Oil Corporation, New York
Oates, James F., Jr. Chairman
    Equitable Life Assurance Society of the United States, N.Y.
*Palmer, H. Bruce President
    National Industrial Conference Board, New York
Patton, Thomas F. Chairman
    Republic Steel Corporation, Cleveland
*Peterson, Rudolph A. President
    Bank of America National Trust and Savings Association, San Francisco
Rauch, R. Stewart, Jr. President
    Philadelphia Saving Fund Society, Philadelphia
Roche, James M. Chairman
    General Motors Corporation, Detroit
*Rockefeller, David Chairman
    The Chase Manhattan Bank, N.A., New York
Romnes, Haakon I. Chairman
    American Telephone and Telegraph Company, New York
Rouse, James W. President
    The Rouse Company, Baltimore
Ruder, William President
    Ruder and Finn, Inc., New York
*Sarnoff, Robert W. President
    Radio Corporation of America, New York
Saunders, Stuart T. Chairman
    Pennsylvania-New York Central Transportation Company, Inc., Philadelphia
Schoenhofen, Leo H. President
    Container Corporation of America, Chicago
Spahr, Charles E. President
    The Standard Oil Company (Ohio), Cleveland
Spater, George A. President
    American Airlines, Inc., New York

Spaulding, Asa T. Consultant
        North Carolina Mutual Life Insurance Company, Durham, N.C.
*Stanton, Frank President
        Columbia Broadcasting System, Inc., New York
Steiniger, Edward L. Chairman
        Sinclair Oil Corporation, New York
Stern, Edgar B., Jr. President
        Royal Street Corporation, New Orleans
Sulzberger, Arthur O. President
        The New York Times Company, New York
Thompson, Rupert C., Jr. Chairman
        Textron, Inc., Providence, R. I.
Uihlein, Robert A., Jr. Chairman and President
        Jos. Schlitz Brewing Company, Milwaukee
Valenti, Jack J. President
        Motion Picture Association of America, Inc., New York
*Watson, Thomas J., Jr. Chairman
        International Business Machines Corporation, Armonk, N.Y.
Weinberg, Sidney J. Partner
        Goldman, Sachs and Company, New York
Whitney, John H. Senior Partner
        J. H. Whitney and Company, New York
Wilson, Joseph C. Chairman
        Xerox Corporation, Rochester, New York
Wynne, Angus G., Jr. President
        Great Southwest Corporation, Arlington, Texas

*Member, Board of Directors

139

BCA INFORMAL ADVISORY COMMITTEE

Fred Armstrong
Director of Research and Projects
United States Steel Foundation
New York, New York

Robert J. Buzbee
Director
Education Programs
The Sears-Roebuck Foundation
Skokie, Illinois

Arthur M. Doty
Executive Director
The Alcoa Foundation
Pittsburgh, Penn.

Kenneth R. Ford
Donations and Contributions Counselor
Standard Oil Company of California
San Francisco, Calif.

William F. Leonard
Director of Corporate Relations
Olin Mathieson Chemical Corporation
New York, New York

James L. Macwithey
Director of Public Relations
Bristol-Myers Company
New York, New York

W. S. Markham, Jr.
Vice President
Burlington Industries, Inc.
Greensboro, North Carolina

John Meekin
Public Relations Officer
The Chase Manhattan Bank, NA
New York, New York

Maurice D. Quinlan
Public Relations Manager
American Telephone and Telegraph Company
New York, New York

H. Henry Ramm
Vice President and General Counsel
R. J. Reynolds Tobacco Company
Winston-Salem, North Carolina

A. N. Scallon
Manager
Corporate Support Programs
International Business Machines Corporation
Armonk, New York

W. Homer Turner
Vice President and Executive Director
United States Steel Foundation, Inc.
New York, New York

Walter M. Upchurch, Jr.
Senior Vice President
Shell Companies Foundation, Inc.
New York, New York

Earl B. Whitcraft
Assistant Secretary
Mobil Oil Corporation
New York, New York

John H. Watson, III
Manager
Department of Company Contributions
Division of Public Affairs Research
National Industrial Conference Board
New York, New York

BUSINESS COMMITTEE FOR THE ARTS

OFFICERS

Chairman—C. Douglas Dillon
President—Goldwin A. McLellan
Vice President—Herbert P. Patterson
Secretary—H. Bruce Palmer
Assistant Secretary—Martha Gerken
Treasurer—Devereux C. Josephs

EXECUTIVE COMMITTEE

C. Douglas Dillon
H. Bruce Palmer
Devereux C. Josephs

INDEX